# HOW TO
# LITTER-TRAIN
# HOARDING PACK-RATS!

# HOW TO
# LITTER-TRAIN
# HOARDING PACK-RATS!

*Doris Bennett*

authorHOUSE®

*AuthorHouse*™
*1663 Liberty Drive*
*Bloomington, IN 47403*
*www.authorhouse.com*
*Phone: 1-800-839-8640*

*Published by AuthorHouse    04/05/2013*

*ISBN: 978-1-4772-9833-6 (sc)*

# CONTENTS

# Dedication

I dedicate this book to my wonderful garage selling [and buying] family, neighbors and friends for their years of endless sweat loyalty, love and encouragement.

A very special thanks goes to my hoarding, pack-rat hubby, who made this all possible. Without him, there would never have been a vital, therapeutic need for writing this book in the first place.

**LA VITA LOCO PACK RATS!**

**OLE!**

**LOVE YOU ALL!**

Doris Bennett

# THE PACK-RAT'S PRAYER

OH LORD! Please help me to allow open space to remain that way . . . open!

Help me to resist the overwhelming temptation to cover the top of every flat surface with something.

Give me the strength to fight my hoarding and cluttering demons by putting things away instead of hiding or stacking them.

Protect me from my worst enemy, myself, for I am weak and in great need of your Devine guidance in the ways of order and neatness.

Dear Lord, take my hand and guide me . . . to a waste paper basket, garbage can and recycle bins.

Help me to find my way through my junk packed garage, disorganized cupboards, stuffed, musty closets and dresser drawers!

Guide me to the city dump, and please, stop me from bringing home way more than I take.

Help me resist stacking and piling junk mail, old magazines and newspapers on tables, chairs and in every open space.

Stop me from asking my neighbors to rent me their old sheds or empty garages to store my stuff.

Forgive me for renting self storage units to hide my stuff out of sight until I have the time to sort through it. Because we both know Lord, I never will.

Dear Lord! Show me a sign, a great big, red, white and black sign, that says "Garage Sale!" And help me to accept this 'sign' as the true path to my eternal, and spiritual salvation.

Teach me the wisdom of your words oh Lord, "an eye for an eye," so I may find the common sense to throw out something old before I buy something new!

Teach me to let go, so I may walk through the valley of my life, without falling off, bumping into or tripping over my nasty, vast hoard of forgotten clutter of useless objects.

Oh Dear Lord, give me the sight to see where I put things and the wisdom to understand why I still have it! For I cannot find anything I need so I always have to buy another.

I beseech thee Dear Lord, to grant my sincere requests and I vow with all my heart to be your devoted servant for all time and eternity. Then I Pray, that my devoted family and friends will give me just one more chance. Again.

AMEN

(A Pack-Rat will stop at nothing to defend his treasures!)

# FOREWORD

## "NOT IN MY GARAGE, YOU'RE NOT!"

My husband Earl called it a financial disaster. I called it a temporary inconvenience. Our family and friends called it, the loveliest Mission Garden wedding they had ever been to. One thing is certain it marked the real beginning of my serious garage selling adventures.

Having five sons but only one daughter, it had been my lifelong dream to give my only daughter a big, beautiful, memorable wedding someday, so I did.

Maybe I did go a teeny bit overboard in the budget department. But I worked full-time too. So I cleaned out my savings and borrowed the rest from my credit union.

I admitted that we would have to give up a few minor luxuries for a while, for example . . . our yearly vacation for the next three summers . . . Ouch! No one was happy about that.

For the life of me, I could not figure out how I would be able to dig myself out of this money hole and build up our vacations savings again. Then I noticed an ad in our local newspaper for a nearby garage sale. Duh!

"Good grief, that's it!" I yelled. "We'll just have a few garage sales!"

"Oh no! Not in my garage, you're not!," he informed me with his famous, you gotta be kiddin' me stare.

You see . . . my husband Earl was a 'pack-rat' and was horrified at the mere mention of losing even one small item from his hoard of priceless treasures. When we got married he did admit he liked to "hang on to stuff." But, a [broken] bean pot he made in first grade . . . the owner's manual for every car he ever owned or rebuilt and, the front tire and fender of the 1939 ford jalopy, his first rebuild, in 1957, which would only go backwards? I don't think he had ever thrown anything away his entire life. Okay, the tiny jar filled with my kid's baby teeth, that's mine.

"I won't even open the garage door," I assured him. "I'll have it in our driveway and front yard. Look around this house and in the garage," I said, "we've got tons and tons of stuff we can sell." my head began to spin with all the possibilities and the scheming I'd have to do to get him to part with anything sellable, but the thought of profits way overruled the risks to my life and limbs.

"You won't make enough to put the slightest dent in the wedding bills," my hoardie-hubby said, clutching his aching head.

Before I continue, I would like to take this opportunity, here and now, to clear up a few nasty rumors which were floating around at the time of our so-called financial disaster', such as . . . PG&E did not insist that we start buying our power by the hour. And, my debit card did not spontaneously combust one day at Safeway. But I will admit that

I heard that Bloomingdales may have circulated a memo around the store, with my picture on it, with orders to the sales staff to destroy my credit card on sight if I ever attempted to use it in their store again.

The only thing I do regret is the loan to pay off the wedding expenses lasted much longer than the marriage did. Oh well, you can't win 'em all.

Nevertheless, I forged onward with my plan to makeup the money I spent on the wedding and within the next six months I had or participated in at least a dozen weekend garage sales, making not only enough to pull us out of our financially disastrous money hole but enough for us to go on vacation after all! So there!

The first month of my garage selling my hubby wouldn't speak to me . . . but when he saw the fists-full of money I was raking in he was not only speechless, but started participating by directing sales by adding his own ideas and, more and more of his own treasures to my garage-sale inventory each weekend. Best of all, he stopped his 'woe is me' complaining. To say the least, I was very thankful for that.

After all the excitement died down, I realized that I was really hooked on garage sales, hopelessly and passionately hooked. When my hubby finally did get into the act, he was hooked too and even outselling me sometimes. When that happened, he would gloat shamelessly like he invented garage sales!

The only problem with him helping out was, when there were other garage sales nearby, he was always their best customer. (You wouldn't believe some of the deals he made!) He was a shopoholic, he loved to shop and buy stuff, but never bothered to use or fix whatever he bought. And thank goodness he never remembered what he bought, why or where he bought it. So it was pretty easy to recycled his 'deals,' for a tidy profit at our own garage sales. He never noticed, he was just having way too much fun buying and selling.

READ ON, MAKE MONEY! BUT MAINLY, STAY COOL AND HAVE A BLAST!

# CHAPTER 1

## How To Litter Train Your Hoarding Pack-Rat

In order to maintain your sanity while living under the same roof with a hoarding pack rat, you must come to terms with your priorities. You must sit down and decide what is most important in your life.

If your "better half" is an incurable hoarder or 'collector,' you really have only two choices: neatness or money. If you chose neatness, you can try to cure your pack rat completely of holding onto useless junk and a big good luck to you with that. But you'll have to think very carefully about the consequences of a complete cure. You'll never have anything to sell.

If you opt for the money, you'll have to began training your pack rat right away in the unselfish joys of sharing (for a tidy profit of course!)

I would recommend training your pack rat to share, but pack-rats find it almost Impossible to do so willingly, so you'll have a lot of hard work ahead of you.

There is, I will now point out, a way to find neatness and profit. It isn't easy, but it does have its rewards. It's called "throw-away" therapy and it's my own little technique for making the most out of life, living with a pack rat.

## Step 1:

First you must get the pack rat's complete confidence by sitting them down (in a tidy atmosphere, if you can find one) for a calm discussion about the benefits and blessings that are heaped upon those who cease their anti-neatness [messy] lifestyle (and quit using your home and garage as the city's unofficial trash and garbage dump).

## Step 2:

This step adds guilt therapy. Tell them that, in your book, a neat person is an uncontested candidate for sainthood. Then you dwell upon the pack rat's charming qualities, like their loving personality, devotion, and intelligence. Stress how they use logic so wisely (and compliment them on their big green eyes and their sparkling, sexy smile . . . if you're really getting desperate).

## Step 3:

Now . . . tell them that with all their positive qualities in mind and after very careful consideration, you have come to only one possible, logical conclusion, and that is that any item the pack rat does not put away and instead carelessly tosses must be an item the pack rat (a) no longer needs, (b) no longer wants, (c) no longer respects, or (d) wants destroyed and out of their life and sight forever.

Now here's where you come in for the kill. You inform the pack rat that in the future you will be more than happy to continue cleaning up and picking up after them (the way you have been all along, in case no one has noticed) but that from now on, when you do, you will have the option of disposing of each and every discarded item in any manner that you and you alone see fit.

## Step 4:

When you reach this point in your therapy, you will have to be very, very careful so the pack rat will not catch on. You see, you tell them that you choose to throw away the items, but the truth is that you will not be throwing them away but putting them into your cleverly hidden garage-sale "litter box." After a respectable length of time has passed, your litter box should be brimming over with delicious goodies. Don't worry, your pack rat won't have the guts to ask you about any of the missing items. (they were warned, right? My motto is, if they don't miss it, they don't need it!)

## Step 5:

The next big step is to haul it all to a friend's garage sale (preferably in another part of town) and rake in all that luscious green stuff! Just don't get caught! If your pack rat ever found out that you were getting rich off their littering phobia, they'd definitely demand a piece of the action!

Pack rats are greedy little critters. That's why they are pack rats. They want it all and all for nothing. There's only three little words in pack rat's vocabulary: free, mine and money!

This method should cure your anxiety about your pack rat's littering, because you're getting rich. But they'll have to wise-up sooner or later when they start running out of things, stuff and junk. Again, I warn you, teaching a pack rat to pick up after himself or herself, put things away in their proper place, and throw out what's no longer in use or needed, will cut short your thriving garage-sale career. The only good point is a neater, cleaner house.

But if you are stuck with a pack rat who is as stubborn as an old mule and you want them to clean up their act permanently, then I strongly urge you to begin training your pack-rat in the joys of sharing, that I mentioned earlier.

## Step 6:

This step is based on honor-system therapy. Having only one step, it's not nearly as much fun as the previous technique, but it's quite effective. There's no sneaking around in this one. The sharing approach is direct and honest. But, to keep it interesting I've added a wee touch of torture just for flavor, by putting your intentions right under their noses!

Here's what you do: go into the family room, stand directly in front of the TV, during primetime of course, to get everyone's undivided attention—and announce loud and clear, "Hear ye! Hear ye! Attention, all personnel! To whom it may concern, and you know who you are! All items not returned after use to their properly assigned storage compartment, drawer, or closet will henceforth from this day forward be subject to confiscation and automatic confinement in the garage sale litter-box! And, if said items are not claimed within two weeks, I repeat, fourteen days, all items will be sold, I repeat, sold, at my next garage sale! And, (I'm not finished yet!) Any item or items that return to the garage sale litter box after they have been previously claimed twice before, I repeat, twice before, will automatically be considered mine on their third return. And, I will keep all the money that I get for them, I repeat, all the money! Got it? Good!

If this method doesn't do the trick and completely cure your pack rats, you have my sympathy. However, take heart, look on the bright side. This means that you will become the richest and most famous garage-sale Guru in your whole entire neighborhood! Just like me!

## Step 7:

What sharing therapy sometimes accomplishes is that your pack rats now sees how successful your garage sales have become as a result of their bad habits and get so jealous that they insist on a piece of the action for themselves. They'll try to do you out of your rightful profit by offering to voluntary contribute . . . to their own litter-box. WAIT! You don't want them cleaning out their closets and dresser drawers and tossing out all the good stuff you just bought for them. The rules are, it can only be things they have outgrown, can't wear, don't need, out dated, in workable condition, in good shape, clean and reusable. Then they can have a litter box all their own. Wall-la! Neatness will reign when they realize that if all their 'litter' has been money in the your pocket, then let it be money in their own pocket. This does cut into your profits considerably, but litter-training your pack-rats is the main issue here. Right?

## Step 8:

Pack rats are notoriously sneaky critters, and you may catch them sticking their little paws where they don't belong once the garage-sale bug bites them. So do keep the rest of the family's garage-sale boxes safely hidden but handy to them all around the house. You could put names on them. If you want one big family litter box in the garage, from which the rest of the family will share equal profit, be sure to keep an eye on its contents, at all times. True pack rats all tend to be not only sneaky but very private creatures as well. Their own litter box will most likely be hidden away somewhere where it's dark and musty. It wouldn't hurt to insist on checking its contents once in a while too, if things are mysteriously vanishing from the family litter box.

## Step 9:

**About the litter-box.** In my opinion no family should ever be without one. It should be a standard part of every home training program to teach children the joys of a litter-less, clean, and healthy environment. They learn to have pride in themselves, respect for a hard-earned dollar and, most importantly, that if they don't pick up after themselves, mommy will sell their things right out from under their cute little freckled noses.

It stands to reason that a litter box should be large, roomy, and have "garage-sale litter box" printed in large letters clearly visible on the sides and top. We wouldn't want anyone to throw things into the wrong litter box, now would we? Especially if you just happen to own a cat, not labeling the litter box properly could cause a very unpleasant problem. If your kitty can read, that is. Well, Garfield can!! I swear mine could read the flavors on his cat food can, too.

We used to own a big white tomcat named W.C. (for white cat). Well, I thought it was a clever name! He couldn't stand being left out of anything that was going on around the house. The garage sale litter-box was off-limits to him, which made him crazy. So he thought that he'd use his own!!

W.C. was forever "collecting" small items around the house. If it would fit into his mouth, he would instantly bury it. Need I tell you where? He alone broke the entire family of leaving small objects lying around the house. Believe me, if you have to go digging in a cat's litter-box to look for your favorite necklace, watch, or earrings [ugh!] you learn pretty darn fast to put things away, that's for sure!

## Step 10: Last but not least . . .

Listen to the voice of years of experience. Try this litter-training therapy on your pack rats. You have nothing to lose but tons of litter, and the peace of mind of life in an uncluttered world to gain. All you need to remember is be patient and make sure your pack rat's litter-box is kept clean and dry at all times. Be sure to give them lots of TLC and plenty of attention, when they deserve it. Show them a 'garage sale' sign whenever they misbehave and give them treats when they are good. Stroke them tenderly when they're lonely and feed them at least twice a day, you will have a very happy pack rat purring around your house, and using their "litter-box" for the rest of your (wealthy garage selling) life! Wait a minute . . . am I talking about humans or cats? I forgot, but these tips work the same for either!

# CHAPTER 2

# THE GARAGE-SELLER'S SURVIVAL KIT

It's a nice sunny morning. Your garage sale is all set up, everything's in place and ready to go. You look at your watch. Zero hour is only five minutes away. Just outside your closed garage door, the familiar sounds of anxious breathing mingles with the murmur of hushed, eager voices. The moment is getting closer and closer. Your senses sharpen, your mind springs to life, and your heart begins to flutter wildly.

Bracing your feet firmly on the ground, your inhale deeply, square your shoulders, and prepare yourself. You check your money apron with both hands, with the confidence of a lawman going into battle to save his town, reassuring himself that his six-shooters are ready.

Now all there is left to do is wait. You check your watch again: only three more minutes to go. Then the garage doors will be opened and you will be standing there face to face with them—the pushing, shoving, merciless mob of garage-sale buyers. Two minutes more. You can handle it. One minute more. Thirty seconds. You nod your head, giving the signal to open the doors. You're ready for anything, any kind of emergency. No matter what might happen, you'll be able to meet it bravely, head on, because clutched firmly in your quaking grasp is your priceless, life-saving, garage-seller's survival kit.

This probably sounds familiar to you? No? If not, it's because you've never had a garage sale! So heads up and I will let you in on my best-kept secret of successful garage-selling. Come close now and pay attention, for I am about to give away my very best trick of the trade, a way of making a long, hard day of garage-selling easier, much more profitable, and nearly painless. In the middle of a busy garage sale, you just don't have time to drop everything and dash into the house to get something you need or forgot. To make sure that I had everything I needed with me at all times, one day I sat down and made a list of things to have handy. Then I gathered all the things on the list together and put them into a big, roomy tote bag. It didn't take me long to realize how indispensable that tote bag full of odds and ends and supplies had become, not only to me but to many of my absent-minded fellow garage-sellers as well. I started calling it my survival kit.

This kit has turned out to be an indispensable tool for the truly organized garage sale, worth it's weight in gold. I personally would never have a garage sale without it. To be truthful, I couldn't have a garage sale without it.

What I carry in my kit may sound a wee bit unusual or maybe even a little weird to you. But to me each and every item has a meaning and usefulness all its own. I have learned the hard way, and now I can share my prized secret with you.

You don't have to fill your survival kit with the same things that I put in mine. We all have different needs and tastes. The area in which you live can have a bearing on what goes into it as well. What you'll find in mine will simply give you an idea or two and some helpful hints or guidelines to work with when you start putting together your own survival kit.

Here what I have in my garage seller's survival kit:

## Item #1: Small clipboard, notepad, and pen or pencil

I hated lugging around a heavy, cumbersome adding machine all the time, because, in the first place, I never seemed to be anywhere near an electric outlet. Second, I would be bombarded with offers to buy it all the time whenever a buyer spotted the darn thing. I knew that I'd probably end up selling it someday, so I finally did.

My mini-calculator was always getting lost [or sold] in all the fuss and muss of my busy garage sales, and besides, I'd never had one that was dependable anyway. The dang battery cells would usually go stone dead when I needed it most, right in the middle of adding up a sale.

When my last mini-calculator pooped out on me, I was forced out of necessity into using old paper bags, with my eyebrow pencil or a crayon to add everything up and keep track of all my sales. Then in the rush of things, I'd end up giving that very same bag away by mistake to hold a customer's purchase, thus wiping out a whole day's worth of bookkeeping.

Keeping a clipboard, pad and pencil on hand and is definitely the safest and least stressful way to go.

## Item #2: Colored stickers and labels for pricing:

If it's a group sale, make sure that no other seller at your garage sale is using the same color stickers and labels as you are for your price-marking. I don't care how good a friend you are with the other seller. When money is involved, friendship flies right out the window and that monster of greed flies back in to take its place every time.

If any sale items get mixed, you won't be able tell what is whose in a buyer's clutches. And one of the other seller's might think that you're snitching a few of her sales, by mistake of course. Believe me, you'll be dueling in the sun, challenged to broom handles at thirty paces, high noon behind the small-appliance table. I know my garage-sellers. Money first, friendship later!

## Item #3: Head gear and sunglasses

I say "head gear" because I carry five different kinds with me. One for sun, one for rain, one for wind, a miner's hat with a head lamp, and a crash helmet!

You see, I live in an area in the good ol' U.S. of A that is a weatherman's paradise (or nightmare, depending on how good he is at flipping a coin), the alive and well notoriously great San Francisco bay area.

Weathermen come here from all over the world for their boot camp training! Their final exam is correctly predicting Bay Area weather for seven straight days, in a row. If they can pass that test, they will be presented with the weatherman's sharpshooter's medal and the coveted place of honor for all time and eternity in the weathermen's hall of fame! So far no weatherman has ever earned that medal or even an honorable mention. But they do keep trying, deftly misleading us year after year. I used to wonder why we had the same weathermen here for as long as I can remember. Now I realize that they're eternally in training, rather like doctors, I think, who are forever "practicing" medicine.

Bay area television stations have spent millions of dollars on high-tech weather satellite gobbledy-gook just to be able to tell you whether you should wash your car or water your lawn the next day, and they still can't second-guess mother nature. The sanity, stress, and lifespan of a bay area weatherman is nearly half that of an air traffic controller, and the controllers have to depend almost entirely on reports from the weathermen!

The only job requirements needed for a weatherman here are being able to count to seven so they can read the seven-day forecast, having a lifetime membership in the FCC (finger-crosser's club), and knowing how to use a pointed stick safely without hurting themselves or ripping a hole in the weather map.

This is the only place on the face of the earth where the weather has broken both the highest and the lowest recorded temperatures, in the same week! Sometimes I feel as though I'll keel over from heat stroke just trying to keep my fingers and toes from getting frostbite.

In this area it's much safer to wear all five pieces of headgear at once, like I do sometimes, just to be on the safe side. First my sun hat, in case the sun decides to chase away the drizzle clouds. Then I put on my rain hat, in case the sun can't catch them in time. Then I tie it all down with my wind scarf so my hats won't blow away while the wind tries its best to beat them both to the punch! Then, if that famous San Francisco fog decides to stay around for the garage sale, I'm ready for that too! On goes my miner's hat and with a flick of a switch I have my own fog lamp. Boy, is that handy to light my way around. You've got to be ready for anything at all times. True-blue veteran garage-sale buyers would never let a little pea-soup fog stop 'em!

At last, but not by any means least, the crash helmet. (I know that one's been making you crazy!)

Around the San Francisco Bay Area, you don't have to go to all the trouble of falling in love to make the earth move for you! We just wait around for mother nature to get into one of her bored and restless moods. That's when she likes to throw us a little playful surprise party, in the form of a rib-tickler called an earthquake. Earthquakes are mother nature's favorite, sneaky form of a practical joke, because you can't see one coming on a satellite weather map, you can't smell or taste it in the air, you can't feel it coming, because if you do . . . forget-a-'bout it, it's already here! And the only weathermen who are smart enough to predict them can't even speak English or any other language for that matter . . . because they're animals. Trust me . . . when my cat starts spinning in circles, races full speed around the walls, then hides under my bed. I pay attention!!!

"Why does everybody blame me for all the earthquakes?" asks mother nature. "they're not my fault, they're San Andreas!"

Oh yes, the sunglasses. They're for obvious reasons (so no one will recognize the idiot wearing all that ridiculous head gear!)

## Item #4: munchies

Having a garage sale is more than just a way of making some extra money. It's also a great reason to get together with some fun friends and pig out on munchies. I know some people (not to name any names, of course) who bring more munchies to a garage sale to eat than they bring stuff to sell! Their survival kits contain enough calories to ward off months of snack attacks—or to hold them over until the next garage sale.

I'm always dieting—between garage sales! I have to! I would never dream of offending any of my fellow garage-sellers by refusing to share some of their yummy, homemade goodies. What kind of friend do you think I am, anyway? Boy, that's a good one.

MUSIC PUTS PEOPLE IN A BUYING MOOD.

## Item #5: A portable radio, iPod or CD player:

These are a must-have item. No true garage seller should ever be caught without at least one of them. As in any upscale store where you plan to spend your hard earned money, there must be an atmosphere of feel-good background music all around you to put you into a pleasant, [buying] mood. However, I have been known to sell my portable radio or CD player when that 'greedy-bug' bites me. But only when the price is right, of course.

## Item #6: Money box and a money apron:

I never take my money apron off, I might sell it! I was offered five dollars for my own garbage can. It still had our garbage in it, and I took the money! I was offered fifty cents for the sweater I was wearing. If I hadn't been so offended by the fifty-cent offer, I would have taken it right off my back, then and there, and handed it over!

I don't need any of my friends doing me in. I do a good enough job all by myself.

## Item #7: Sewing kit (including scissors):

There is no doubt in my mind that I will have some last-minute button-tightening, hem-tacking, or seam-mending to do on some of the clothes I have up for sale, so I always keep a little sewing kit handy in my survival kit.

I can remember a dress I once put up for sale. I never seemed to find the time to fix the hem, so I decided to sell it as is. A nice lady wanted to buy it, but she said she'd pay me an extra dollar for the dress if I'd fix the hem for her. Wow! An extra dollar! How could I refuse? So I fixed it and sold the forty-five-dollar dress to her for five dollar, plus the extra dollar for putting in the hem! (I can't believe I really did that, but I did.)

## Item #8: Black or red felt pen, white or colored poster paper:

If sales are slow, I like to make some sale signs for some of my merchandise or some eye-catching little posters to set around. Making these little signs for the other sellers keeps me quite busy too, because I'm usually the only one who thought of bringing the materials. I make little posters that say "if you don't like our prices . . . dicker!" or "all items on this table $1.00 each." The reason I state "on this table" is because I had a sign on a table once that read "everything $1.00." I soon had two women fighting over the card table that I was using to set the merchandise on, and another pulling the sheet off the table, that I was using as a cover, thinking that I was selling them for a dollar as well. I still get offers for the tables and covers anyway. People will try to buy anything.

## Item #9: Transparent, duct or masking tape, stapler, tacks, and hammer:

The tape is to hold my signs in place, if I want to be sure they will stay right where I put them. The stapler is for the ones that the tape won't hold. If that can't do the job on the real stubborn suckers, out come the hammer and tacks!

If a price sticker, label, or sign decides to float away and land on something not in your garage-sale inventory, you'll have pure mayhem on your hands every time. I had five tree roses still in their five-gallon cans end up with a stray one-dollar price tag on them at a garage sale of mine. I hadn't discovered the problem until a nice little old lady brought me a five-dollar bill and asked if I would deliver "the beautiful rose trees" to her house just down the street! I'm lucky she didn't ask us if we'd plant them in her yard too. (no, I didn't sell her my rose trees for five dollars.)

One time I noticed a man hungrily sizing up my driveway, until I quickly snatched up the thirty-five-dollar sign that had fallen off the side of a three-drawer filing cabinet I had up for sale. That poor man looked so disappointed when if picked up that sign! I've always wondered what would he have done with it if I had sold it to him? I wouldn't take a penny less than one hundred dollars for it anyway.

## Item #10: Garage sale guest list:

If you are a real pro garage-seller, which means that you either have or go to more than two garage sales a year, people get to know you as a garage seller with dependable merchandise. Some garage-sale junkies wouldn't miss a good garage sale if they could help it for any reason in the world, short of nuclear holocaust. And even then, they would be the first to line to look over the pickin's if there were anything left to pick over!

These are the ones that would be glad to sign your "guest list". This list is actually a mailing list so you can send these people a card or a flyer telling them about your next garage sale or about one that you will be selling at.

## Item #11: Folding chair, clip-on beach umbrella, and two card tables:

Yes! I know, these things will not fit into your tote bag, but nonetheless I consider them part of my survival kit. If you are going to someone else's home to sell some things, you cannot take it for granted they will be able to furnish you with a place to sit in the shade and tables to put your merchandise on. When I'm invited to sell at another's garage sale, I always come fully equipped and prepared. (and I'm fun to have around because I like to make silly signs to put on the tables.) In a nutshell, here's what's in my survival kit, let's look at what we've got:

#1.  —SMALL CLIPBOARD, NOTE PAD & PEN OR PENCIL.

#2.  —COLORED STICKERS AND LABELS.

#3.  —HEAD GEAR AND SUNGLASSES.

#4.  —MUNCHIES

#5.  —PORTABLE RADIO, iPOD OR CD PLAYER.

#6.  —MONEY BOX & MONEY APRON.

#7.  —SEWING KIT

#8.  —FELT PENS & POSTER PAPER.

#9.  —TAPE, STAPLER, SCISSORS, TACKS, AND SMALL HAMMER.

#10. —GARAGE SALE GUEST LIST.

#11. —FOLDING CHAIR, BENCH UMBRELLA AND CARD TABLES.

# CHAPTER 3

## YOUR GARAGE SALE:
## BUSINESS VENTURE OR THERAPY?

For me, garage sales represented a fabulous way to kill many birds with one stone: build up a shrunken 401K, retirement fund, Christmas account or mad-money account and [my favorite] clear away eons of musty, dusty litter. However, garage sales can mean different things to different people. Besides making extra money and being a whole lot of fun, garage sales are:

**PRACTICAL:** Almost every family on the planet has some sort of pack—rat in its ranks. Even if they don't have one hoarding every seemingly useless item in sight, believe me, it is next to impossible for even the most clean, neat and organized people not to accumulate a few useless, sellable items, once in a while. Garage sales and recycling are nature's way of making closets, garages, and cupboards available by helping you to get rid of all that useless stuff! Even pack-rats can't fool mother nature!

**PROFITABLE:** Interested in a new hand bag, boots, fishing pole, iPod, etc., but unable to scrape together the cash? Well, the item you desire may be no further away than a weekend garage sale. A garage sale can bring you quick and easy profits—pure profit—from the items you no longer want, need, use, or enjoy. No-no-no, take that price tag off your old BF! Shame on you! He wouldn't bring that much anyway.

**GOOD EXERCISE:** If you spend your workweek sitting down, a wild-and-crazy weekend garage sale can be a great way to get a little excitement and exercise back into your boring life. Believe me, all that bending and reaching and jumping around—not to mention the oh-so-strenuous part of counting the money—will get you smiling again and back in shape in no time at all! Trust me!

FORGET HIGH-PRICED HEALTH SPAS! A GARAGE SALE CAN
BE LIKE GETTING *PAID* TO EXERCISE! IT'S FUN, TOO!

# CHAPTER 4

## ALL THE GREAT REASONS TO GET INTO THE BUSINESS

**A GREAT WAY TO MEET NEW FRIENDS:** Singles' bars, online dating, and the like can't hold a candle to the meetin' people power of garage sales. Garage sales can help you get reacquainted with old friends and new neighbors. Plus, you'll meet all kinds of new and interesting people, even a few out-there, quirky ones now and then to boot!

**THERAPEUTIC:** Believe it or not, the hectic hustle, bustle, fun atmosphere of a garage sale can be very therapeutic. The liveliness, the sunshine and the extra income all combine to form positive ions in the air all around you. It's very hard to be depressed when you're making great deals, counting dollars and making new friends.

For whatever reason you begin your garage sale business, remember that the most important thing is to have a good time. Smile! Enjoy. Make a block party out of it! Serve refreshments. Popcorn and store brand pop won't break you and is very welcome on a hot sunny day.

**Tip:** I always have [beer size] plastic cups of pop corn, lots of lollipops or balloons on sticks for the darling kiddies. This will keep their tiny little mouths busy and their cute little hands occupied. Sometimes I'll have a 'kiddies FREE box' of little trinkets and toys. Little kids always love a petting zoo of bugs, worms and goldfish in plastic bottles, and a playpen full of puppies and kittens. Kids will drag their mom and dad to your garage sale to see puppies and get a free lollipop!

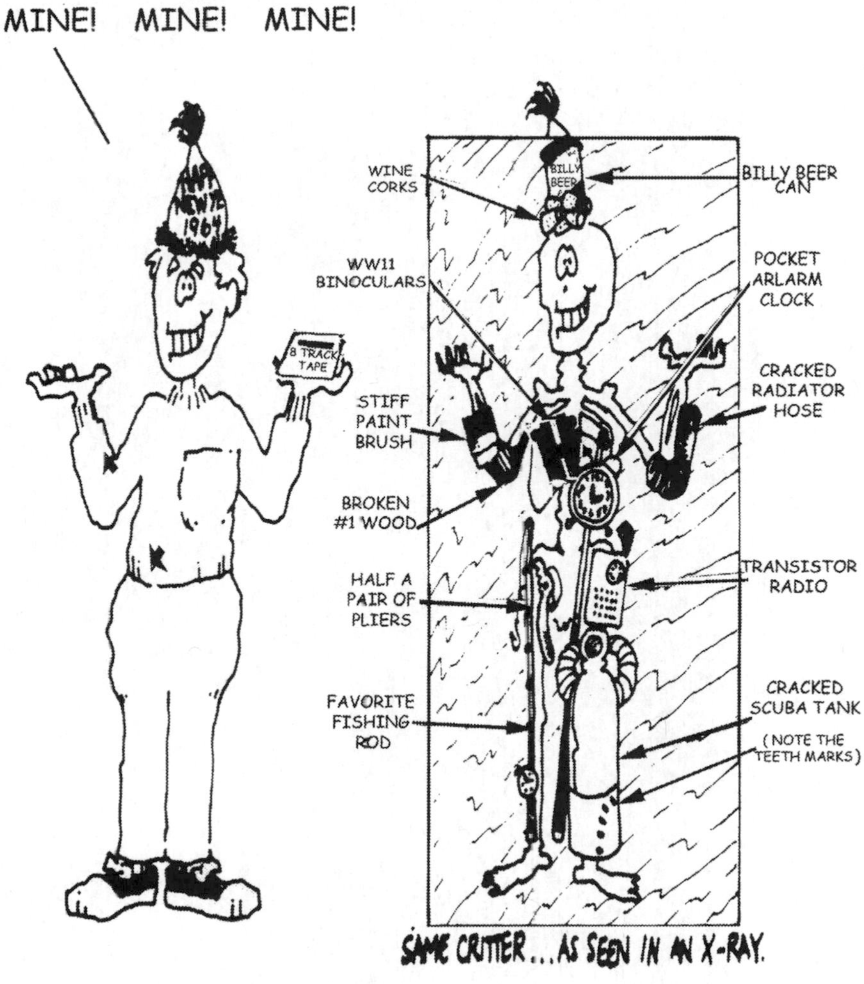


# A NORMAL, EVERYDAY PACK-RAT

# CHAPTER 5

# IS THERE A HOARDING PACK-RAT IN YOUR LIFE?

### HOW YOU CAN TELL? . . .
### WHAT IS A HOARDER OR A PACK-RAT, ANYWAY?

According to WEBSTER'S NEW COLLEGIATE DICTIONARY (p. 816) a **PACK RAT** is:

"1: . . . a large, bushy-tailed rodent (neotama cinerea) of the rocky mountain area that has well-developed cheek pouches and hoards food and miscellaneous objects."

Well, I don't know about yours, but mine doesn't look anything like that—and I don't think he's ever seen the rockies. They did get the hoarding part right, though. Let's look a little further:

According to WEBSTER'S NEW COLLEGIATE DICTIONARY a **HOARDER** is:

One who compulsively collects or hoards secretly, typically large quantities of unneeded or useless items, also food or money. Hoarders have a very difficult time getting rid of anything they feel has value. Hoarders typically have the [treatable] mental disability-disorder called OCD.

AH-HA! Now that sounds just like the critter living in my house!

# CHAPTER 6

## HOW TO MARRY A PACK RAT [?]

There is only one thing more fun than marrying someone who has lots of money, and that's marrying someone who "collects, clutters or hoards." Especially someone who collects lots and lots of good things that you can sell for lots and lots of . . . money! You can take a little more pride in that fact when you go to sell the items. But how do you go about finding one to marry? For the sake of accuracy, first you have to learn how to spot a "collector" or "hoarder!" Remember, they're not those itsy-bitsy, bushy-tailed rodents!

Spotting the male of the species is easy. He wears clothes with pockets that are stretched out of shape by his old, bulging wallet, or a pocket-protector stuffed with other peoples pens he absentmindedly, 'borrowed.' Notice how thick his wallet is. But don't get too excited. That's not cash that makes it so fat but, old receipts, bits of unreadable clippings, faded out photos and business cards of people who died or retired years ago.

If you're not in a situation where you can check out his pants pockets (they're over the chair? Shame on you!) or his wallet, try to get a look at his car. It will be spotless on the outside, polished to a diamond luster, but the inside of the glove box, trunk and under the seats [after you've picked through the gum and McDonalds wrappers] you can find a veritable gold mine in potential garage sale items. (hoarders and pack-rats like to stash their favorite treasures in weird places. After all, they're named after a scavenger-rodent. So use your imagination when searching.)

The pack rat's home is the same way. It may be the neatest house on the block, on the outside, but on the inside you'll find overstuffed closets, cabinets sagging from excess weight, stack and stacks of magazines and news papers, and a garage packed so full it would take the state's search-and-rescue team a week to find you if you ever get up the courage to go in there.

Spotting a female hoarder is also easy. She usually carries a huge handbag, plus a tote bag (both stuffed). A look inside these bags would reveal pieces of lace, unfinished crocheted potholders, half-knitted sweaters, and so on. Though they may be junk to you, these are items the female pack rat considers priceless and would kill for!

Once inside a female pack rat's home (if you can squeeze in, that is), you will notice that she hasn't thrown anything out since god made dirt. And the arid aroma coming from the kitchen? Sorry, dear, it's not comfort food or muffins. It's freshly-baked dough, plastic crafts, paint thinner and drying ceramics. (Pack rats are often avid hobbyists, too. Everything they hoard is a potential, priceless art piece they intend to sell on eBay.)

So, if you are fortunate enough to have found a pack rat, marry it! Sure, your life will get a little messy at times, but think of all the money you'll make selling their creations and collections. Caution: Pilfer slowly, over time, to prevent your pack rat from experiencing an anxiety attack or going into cardiac arrest when they notice something missing.

Take it from the voice of experience, they may be messy, but they're so darn loveable we don't want to cause them further undo stress. They have enough to deal with. They do mean well, though. GOD BLESS 'EM!

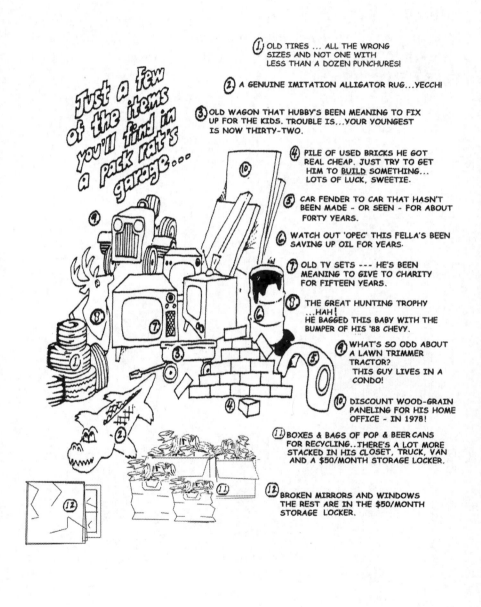

Just a few of the items you'll find in a pack rat's garage...

1. OLD TIRES ... ALL THE WRONG SIZES AND NOT ONE WITH LESS THAN A DOZEN PUNCHURES!

2. A GENUINE IMITATION ALLIGATOR RUG...YECCH!

3. OLD WAGON THAT HUBBY'S BEEN MEANING TO FIX UP FOR THE KIDS. TROUBLE IS...YOUR YOUNGEST IS NOW THIRTY-TWO.

4. PILE OF USED BRICKS HE GOT REAL CHEAP. JUST TRY TO GET HIM TO BUILD SOMETHING... LOTS OF LUCK, SWEETIE.

5. CAR FENDER TO CAR THAT HASN'T BEEN MADE - OR SEEN - FOR ABOUT FORTY YEARS.

6. WATCH OUT 'OPEC' THIS FELLA'S BEEN SAVING UP OIL FOR YEARS.

7. OLD TV SETS --- HE'S BEEN MEANING TO GIVE TO CHARITY FOR FIFTEEN YEARS.

8. THE GREAT HUNTING TROPHY ...HAH! HE BAGGED THIS BABY WITH THE BUMPER OF HIS '88 CHEVY.

9. WHAT'S SO ODD ABOUT A LAWN TRIMMER TRACTOR? THIS GUY LIVES IN A CONDO!

10. DISCOUNT WOOD-GRAIN PANELING FOR HIS HOME OFFICE - IN 1978!

11. BOXES & BAGS OF POP & BEER CANS FOR RECYCLING...THERE'S A LOT MORE STACKED IN HIS CLOSET, TRUCK, VAN AND A $50/MONTH STORAGE LOCKER.

12. BROKEN MIRRORS AND WINDOWS THE REST ARE IN THE $50/MONTH STORAGE LOCKER.

# CHAPTER 7

## THE HOARDING PACK RAT DIAGNOSIS TEST

I AM NOT A PACK RAT. I JUST SAVE THINGS SO I'LL HAVE THEM HANDY WHEN I NEED THEM.

Don't laugh. That poor closet and garage stuffer in your family may really believe what they're saying. They cannot [or will not] admit, even to themselves, that they just might be a victim of the nation's most rampant and contagious disease: Hoardinitis.

This condition is usually hereditary, extremely contagious, life threatening, most annoying and very painful . . . mainly to others. Most victims are completely unaware of their condition.

Hoardinitis has no known cure, but it can be made more bearable for those who must live with the afflicted individual. How? By having garage sales, of course.

Now, for those loved ones of yours who are still stuck in the denial phase, here's a little test guaranteed to reveal their case of Hoardinitis. How will you get them to take this test? Well, tell them that it's a

Smart Shopper's IQ Test! Or, forget it. You can just take the test for them.

**#1: WHEN I SEE A SALE SIGN, I . . .**

A. Ignore it.

B. Make a point to shop there soon.

C. Immediately break out in a cold sweat, my heart racing like a trembling Chihuahua.

**#2 WHEN MY SPOUSE STARTS SPRING-CLEANING, I HELP, AND THINK . . .**

A. "It's about time."

B. Feel that I might have a few things to throw out

C. Panic, lock up my closet, garage, private rooms, and storage shed, and then bury the keys in the rose garden.

**#3: IF MY SPOUSE DECIDES TO HAVE A GARAGE SALE, I . . . think,**

A. "Wow! What a great way to make extra money!"

B. Am uninterested because there's nothing I want to sell.

C. Go into cardiac arrest at the mere thought of selling any of my stuff ie: treasured trinkets.

**#4:** WHEN I GO TO THE CITY DUMP, I . . .

A. Empty the truck or trailer and just return home.

B. Empty the truck or trailer and look around a little.

C. Bring back more than I hauled there, wishing I'd brought the bigger truck.

**#5:** WHEN I GO TO THE SUPER MARKET, I . . .

A. Stick to my shopping list faithfully.

B. Buy a few extra sale things, if I need them.

C. Buy everything on my list plus a case of everything on sale, whether use it or not.

**#6:** WHEN I PASS A TRASH DUMPSTER, I . . .

A. Continue on my merry way, never giving it a second thought.

B. Stop and peek inside, just out of curiosity.

C. Stop, look around to see if anyone is watching, then dive in and dig frantically, taking any item that has the slightest bit of use left in it.

**#7:** AFTER CHRISTMAS, WHEN I GO SHOPPING, I . . .

A. Go simply to exchange gifts.

B. I may catch a few after-Christmas sales.

C. Buy everything on next year's list plus any old Christmas trees that still look healthy.

**#8: WHEN I'M WORKING AROUND THE HOUSE AND NEED A TOOL,**

A. I . . . simply go get it because I always put things away.

B. Go to where I last used it because I never put it away.

C. Couldn't tell you in a million years where I left it last and don't want to take the time to look for it now, so I just go out and buy a new one, and maybe an extra one for good measure.

**#9: MY POCKETS OR PURSE COULD BEST ARE DESCRIBED AS . . .**

A. Empty, except for mothballs.

B. Comfortably pudgy.

C. Missing only a tire iron.

**#10: I AM MOST FOND OF SAYING . . .**

A. "I have a place for everything and everything has its place."

B. "I'll clean up on Tuesday" and then do it on Wednesday.

C. "Neatness sucks!"

When you or your suspected pack rat has finished, give him or her one point for every A choice, five points for every B choice, and ten points for every C choice.

## Type A personality:

If they scored 10 points or less, they're either lying through their teeth or are a type A personality who has no fun at all. Advise them to stop fibbing or loosen up a little, make a mess now and then, do something to prove that they're alive and breathing. If they're telling the truth, they're definitely not suffering from Hoardinitis. This is good news for them but bad news for you and your garage-sale business. (You'll have next to nothing to sell.)

## Type B personality:

If the suspected person scored 11 to 50 points, they may have a dormant or developing case of Hoardinitis. Watch them for more exaggerated symptoms.

## Type C personality:

If the score is 51 to 100, watch out! You have an advanced case of Hoardinitis in the house. The poor dear is incurable, hopeless—and a wonderful source of material for your profitable garage sales! You lucky devil!

## Author's diagnosis

Type C cases are beyond help which means, you will be rich beyond your wildest dreams in no time.

Type A cases are not in need of help, so you can forget about these two groups.

But the type B personality is delicately balanced between total neatness and a junk binge. Watch these people carefully. They are on a precipice. Tomorrow you could either wake up buried in clutter or lying on the floor with all your possessions in the hands of Goodwill. You never know which way they may turn!

Type A's could be reformed type C's and ready to explode. Beware! Treat with caution! They could advance in a blink to type B, which may be the beginning of the end.

# CHAPTER 8

## THE ART AND SCIENCE OF SELLING: THE BEAUTIFUL PEOPLE OF THE GARAGE SALE WORLD

I know there's a lot said about the average this or the average that—even the average person. Let me tell you right now there really is no such thing as an average garage-sale customer, Believe me. They're all unique, and they're all a heck of a lot of fun to deal with.

No matter what you can call it . . . a tag sale, yard sale, bazaar, flea market, junk sale, estate sale or garage sale, they're all the same and buyers want great deals. Your customers can range from seasoned 'Pickers to junk hoarders, and here are just a few of the many types you will be dealing with:

**Harry Hoarder:** this fellow is really just a common pack rat to a more extreme degree. He buys like disaster is at hand. A half bottle of shampoo, 10 year old freeze-dried camping food, and similar items are his favorites.

Caution: Most of the things he's interested in are still in your home and not for sale. Keep him out of the house unless you want him bidding on the half full paper towel roll in your kitchen. And, for heaven sake don't let him get near your bathroom.

**Larry looker:** this guy comes in two varieties: rich and poor. He may be so wealthy that he already has everything his little heart could desire or so monetarily deprived that he can't afford any of your items. Bottom line? He's just there to look.

**Beware:** Mr. Looker is also the one who asks the most questions.

**Diamond Jim Dicker:** Diamond Jim is real professional. He frequents flea markets; bake sales, auto-part sales—any kind of sale he can find—just so he can polish up his dickering skills. Why, he'll take candy from a baby, if he can get the price down low enough. Keep a tight grip on your upper plate or you'll be gumming your t-bone when he gets through with you. He's easy to spot, though, since he's always dressed to the nines, driving a new, foreign sports car, and chomping on a lollipop with a lopsided smile.

**Beware:** Diamond Jim will return again and again, trying to dicker you down in price. Better lock up your daughter.

**Peter Pest:** the major difference between Peter and old Diamond Jim is that Peter Pest always buys something, even if it's weeks and weeks later.

Why do I call Peter a pest? Because he will spot something at your sale that he absolutely must have but will claim your prices are way too high. He will then make you a ridiculously low offer, which you will turn down, and he will walk off in a huff. Mr. Pest will drive around the block, stop at your sale again, and make you another offer. Again you will turn it down and he'll storm off. A week will pass and then he'll ring your doorstep, wanting to know if you still have such-and-such and if he can make you an offer.

Beware: this will go on and on, so my suggestion to you is, let him have the darn thing. Otherwise, you'll never get rid of him or live in peace again.

Earl. E. Bird: Earl is easy to spot. He's your first customer. Yes-sir-ee, he'll be at your door at dawn on the day of your garage sale, determined to get first crack at all the goodies. He may still have his nightcap on his head and his pajamas on underneath his trench coat, but if he remembered to bring his wallet, Eager Earl can be a welcome addition to your garage sale. He's most fond of tools and practical stuff.

Beware: Caution: Mr. Bird usually arrives so early that he's still half asleep. You may have to point him in the direction of his house when it's time for him to leave.

Earl E. Byrd

**Connie Collector:** if it's old, Connie will buy it. But that's understandable, because dear Connie dresses old, thinks old, drives an old car, and worse, expects 1906 prices at your garage sale. She's a loveable little lady, but don't expect to sell her much more than two or three inches of old, yellowed lace.

**Caution:** put up orange construction cones around your car. Connie doesn't see so well and parks about the same.

**Annie Handler:** Annie has been known to unnerve even the most patient of us. She will pick up and inspect everything in sight—her arms out like a hungry octopus—carry the stuff around with her for hours, then decide she doesn't really "need" any of it anyway. When she does buy, the things that most appeal to Annie are faded plastic bowls, rumpled muumuus, perfume, and old, empty gift boxes to store them in. She likes to handle everything, not use it.

**Beware:** it may become necessary to point out to other customers that, yes, the items in Annie's clutches are still for sale.

**Hal Holder:** this guy never brings enough money to a garage sale. What's worse is that Hal will only inform you he left his wallet at home after he's talked down the price of the item he wants. He'll beg you to hold it for him, assuring you he'll be back in a flash. Don't expect him until two minutes before closing.

**Beware:** There's no caution needed if you just learn a very simple trick. When Hal asks, say no, or make him leave his car and walk home for his wallet so he will come back.

**Fran Fussy:** poor Fran, her life is so sad. Nothing is the right color, the right fit—the right height, width, and texture. She will have you sobbing right along with her as she inspects your collection of wrong things. And the questioning: You must have a twenty-seven-inch piece of green velvet ribbon here somewhere, she says. Don't tell her where it is. Allow her the enjoyment of the hunt.

Beware: a lot of Franny's complaining is designed to talk you down in price. Watch out for her.

# CHAPTER 9

## Selling to the public

Effective salesmanship is both an art and a science, believe me. A certain amount of natural talent helps, but there are still plenty of technical tips and tactics that must be learned and developed.

### #1

First and foremost prerequisite to good salesmanship is liking people. After all, no one has yet found a way to have a garage sale without people, so it's important that you have or develop a sociable nature. I grew up in the warm, happy, crazy atmosphere of a large family, the Canovas, and that's probably why it's easy for me to feel right at home in a crowd. (Incidentally, in addition to yours truly, our family produced the late, wonderful hillbilly comedian, Judy Canova, star of movies and radio the '40s, '50s and TV in the '70s)

#2

The most helpful aspect of any neighborhood merchandiser's personality is an abundance of natural energy. "Up" people make fantastic salespeople because everyone gets caught up in their enthusiasm.

While factors one and two must, for the most part, be innate, the following factors can be learned. If you're already a successful wheeler-dealer naturally, you can skip these and get started on setting up your garage sale. But if you're more accustomed to being a customer, take a few minutes to study the rest of this section. Armed with this information, you will become a super salesperson.

#3

Identification (or "whose garage sale is this anyway?")

It is extremely beneficial, profit-wise, to wear an apron, hat, button, or other identifying mark that shows you are the host or hostess. This way people will know who to ask for assistance or who to seek for some serious wheelin' and dealin'.

Once you're outfitted with that special identifying garment, remember to remain visible. Sell that rack of old suits, but don't hide behind it.

#4

Body language (or "you got a license to use those hands?")

Most energetic people are guilty of over-use of the feet, legs, arms, and hands, especially when sales negotiations get hot. And yet it's very important that you limit gesturing and movements. Why? Because they distract people (especially hand movements), make them nervous, and draw attention away from your fantastic, bargain—priced products.

## #5

Eye contact (or "looooook into my eyes!")

At garage sales there are no money-back guarantees, warranties, or exchanges at a later date. People are buying used products, and they're making the decision and sometimes taking a big risk based on the products' appearance and your honest face.

Now, everyone knows that an honest appearance begins with good eye contact. Maintaining eye contact with a customer during the course of a sale is crucial because it adds to your credibility.

## #6

Creating customer involvement (or "she hit me right in the ego!")

Customers are people too, and people have egos. If you want to create a positive environment for sales, then do what ad writers do: use the pronoun "you" as much as possible.

By saying something like "you will love the coffee this pot makes" rather than "I love the coffee this pot makes," you are involving the customer with the product and showing an interest in their life.

# #7

Establishing something in common (or "you mean Dr. Jones is your analyst, too?!")

Right from the start, you should try to find something you and the customer have in common. This can be an affinity for the same color, kids who attend the same school, or any one of a number of seemingly trivial items. Establishing something in common helps relax the customer; you suddenly appear more like a friend and neighbor than just another local merchant. Besides being a great sales tool, finding things you have in common with others is fun and very practical for neighbors.

# #8

Response manipulation (or "I'm the new owner of a what?")

Here we have another high-powered sales technique. Advertising and salespeople refer to it as response manipulation, but I call it "yes-ing." Once you've got the customer yes-ing, he or she will yes their way right to your checkout table.

How does it work?

For example:

"Nice day, isn't it?"
"Sure is."
"Say, isn't your SUV one of those new Fords?"
"Yes, it is.")
"This is a nice vase, don't you think?" (Their response?
"Yes, my wife loves those."

By the way, this technique also works on your kids where homework, room cleaning, and the like are concerned.


## An exercise:

To help you make better sense of these salesmanship techniques and factors, I've designed a mock sales encounter. Locate your spouse, a friend, or any willing assistant, and enlist their help in putting the sales tips to work:

You: "hi there!" (smile even if the only business you've had all day is chucking free popcorn at the neighbor kids.)

Customer: "hello."
Y: "My name's (name) What's yours?"
C: "I'm (name)."
Y: "Well, (name) I guess you'd like to do a little browsing?" (This Takes the pressure off the customer.)
C: "As a matter of fact, yes." (Positive response)
Y: "Great, now promise me you'll holler if you have any questions, Okay?"
C: "Sure." (Positive response)

Later
Y: "How ya doin', (name)? "Lots of interesting items, aren't there?"
C: "Yes, there are." (Positive response)
Y: "That's a super-looking shirt you're wearing. I've been looking for one just like it for myself. Where did you get it?" (Establishing something in common)
C: "At Macy's, I think."
Y: "It's very nice, but isn't it frightening how expensive clothes are these days?"

C: "Yes, it certainly is." (Positive response)

Y: "It really is smarter to buy used clothing. Like this jacket, worn twice and yet I'm selling it for three-fourths off the regular price. Isn't that a great buy?"

C: "Well, yes, yes it is." (Positive response)

Y: "And look at this color. It's so versatile. It goes with everything. Do you own a pair of beige or brown slacks?"

C: "Yes." (Positive response)

Y: "Fantastic! Think what a great addition this will be to your wardrobe. And affordable, too. People will think you paid a lot more for it." (Ego)

C: "It is nice."

Y: "Let's see how it looks on you. There! Isn't that perfect?" (If customer is buying item for him/herself.)

C: "Well, it's a little large."

Y: "Now, now. We can't all be as slim and trim as you. It just needs a touch of tailoring."

C: "I, um, suppose so."

Y: "and besides, it looks so much better on you than it did on the person who said they were coming back for it later. (Ego appeal and added sense of immediacy) But they left no deposit, so I suppose it's all right to let you have it." (This comment is optional.)

C: "Oh good. I'll take it!"

Y: "Great! Your wife/husband is going to be so pleased with the way this jacket looks on you—and what a bargain!"

## The true garage-sale mogul

Don't think for a moment that just because you're not running a high-priced department store you don't need a good sales technique. You do. After all, you're in business.

In fact, the neighboring garage-sale manager needs effective selling habits and ideas more than big-business people. You see, though they have stumbled into your garage sale, Mr. And Mrs. Doe aren't looking for a one-and-a-half-speed blender or pink plastic flamingoes. You must convince them that your products will make their life better, that crushed ice margaritas will taste more authentic in the backyard with pink flamingoes around.

Keep in mind that, in addition to instilling a need in customers for your unique items, you will also be trying to sell a number of common products. It's up to you and your sales expertise to persuade customers to buy your lamp without a shade rather than the lamp without a shade at your neighbor's garage sale.

Sales checklist

1) Be sociable.
2) Get exited.
3) Be visible.
4) Limit hand/body movements. (don't get too excited.)
5) Maintain eye contact.
6) Talk in terms of you, not I.
7) Ask questions that will elicit a positive response.
8) Find something you and the customer have in common.
9) Always remember the importance of a good sales technique.

In other words, study factors one through eight!

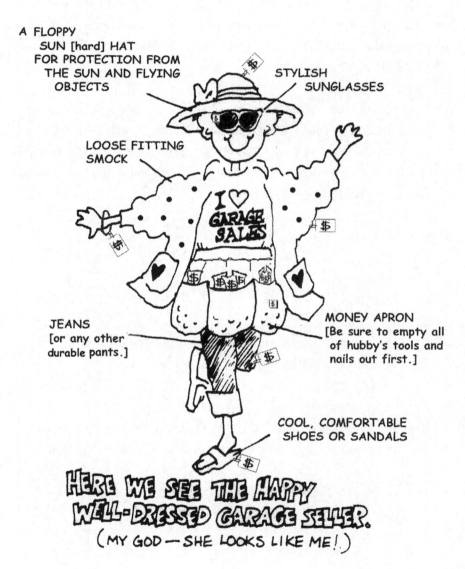

A FLOPPY
SUN [hard] HAT
FOR PROTECTION FROM
THE SUN AND FLYING
OBJECTS

STYLISH
SUNGLASSES

LOOSE FITTING
SMOCK

I ♥ GARAGE SALES

JEANS
[or any other
durable pants.]

MONEY APRON
[Be sure to empty all
of hubby's tools and
nails out first.]

COOL, COMFORTABLE
SHOES OR SANDALS

HERE WE SEE THE HAPPY
WELL-DRESSED GARAGE SELLER.
(MY GOD — SHE LOOKS LIKE ME!)

# CHAPTER 10

## FASHION
## Outfitting the Garage-Sale Entrepreneur

**Function and fashion:**

Whoever said that the garage-sale set was uncouth just didn't know what they were talking about. We're just as "couth" as the next person. Especially when it comes to our meticulously designed fashions.

What does fashion have to do with garage sales? Well, you have to wear something, so it might as well be fashionable—with a little practicality thrown in as well.

The first rule of garage-sale fashion is, of course, comfort, followed by ease of movement, durability, and style.

Whether you wear a burlap sack or a string bikini, make sure that you're comfortable and happy about your choice. Your outfit will help determine the outcome of the whole day. If you're uncomfortable nothing will seem to go right, and when your mood plummets so do your sales!

What? You mean you don't own a smock top? You shouldn't be satisfied wearing one of your husband's old shirts; that's too tacky! If the problem is finding a smock top, I can help.

I have to admit that I kicked myself when my mother came up with this one. She was always wearing a smock top because one of her hobbies was painting. I could never find smocks like hers, so one day I asked her where she bought them. She said, "they're just everyday dusters that I shorten to smock length. If it doesn't have big, patch pockets, I make them from the excess material I cut off."

Now, how could anything be so simple! You can buy dusters, or short housecoats in the women's lingerie section of department stores at the mall, or online. And I thought I never overlooked a trick.

Tip: If you want to save money, buy your dusters, or short housecoats, at a thrift store or a garage sale.

# Chapter 11

## PRODUCTS

**Product popularity: what sells, what doesn't**

Having reached "expert" status in the fine art of garage selling, I think that I can give you my honest opinion of a fair sampling of items that really go at garage sales. I'll start my list with what I feel from experience are the hottest items and end with those that need a big shove before they'll move.

SHOPLIFTERS LOVE CROWDED PLACES,
SO KEEP A CLOSE WATCH ON YOUR BUSINESS.

DO NOT SELL ANYTHING THAT DOESN'T WORK PROPERLY! (AND I MEAN NEVER!)

Tools Sales rating (SR): scalding!

This group includes any kind of tools—especially auto-repair tools—including gardening tools, power or manual lawn mowers and trimmers, carpentry tools, and building equipment like hammers, ladders, paint, nails, and saws. All tools should be placed out front in plain view on the first table that customers will see, with the larger items out on the parking strip. Believe me, tools are traffic-stoppers.

**Auto parts (used) and auto accessories (SR): Scorching!**

This category includes car radios and stereos, motor parts, interior and exterior gadgets and accessories, body parts, and more. Home mechanics are always on the lookout for anything pertaining to autos. People who restore old cars are the greatest scavengers of old parts, so state in your ad what make, model, and year of car you have parts for. If you know you have parts for a classic, don't just mention it in your ad, brag about it. Find out what similar parts are going for, and then reduce your prices for a quick sale.

Auto parts are the best way to attract droves of husbands, with wives in tow, to your garage sales.

**Baby furniture (SR) Sizzling!**

To get the highest price possible, baby furniture should be spotless. If it's broken, repair it. Make it look as good as if you were giving it to a friend. Put it out front and you'll have another traffic-stopper.

**Children and baby clothes** (SR) Hot! Hot! Hot!

Clothes must be spotless, clean, and above all, mended (if they need it). You can price them individually or by the box or bag full. At every garage sale I've ever had or been to, someone has asked for children's or baby clothes. I've never had any left over after a sale.

HOW WELL DO TOOLS SELL?

POOF

GET THE PICTURE?

Toys: (SR) Very Hot!

Toys, big or small, sell quite well at garage sales, but only if they are in safe, A-1 condition. If they do need repairing and can be fixed, fix them. (If you can't, give the toys to a charity that is willing and able to.) You will find that most of your toy-buyers are eager but very selective.

**Small appliances:** (SR) HOT!!

This category is a biggie at garage sales. You can throw just about anything that runs and is small enough to carry in one hand into this category: radios, irons, toasters, hair dryers, etc. But make sure that the item works! Have an extension cord ready to prove it. It's also a good idea (and will help you get more money for items) to clean and polish appliances. If they need batteries, include them or at least have fresh batteries ready for testing. And please don't ever attempt to sell anything that needs repair work without first telling the buyer about it. Be honest. If you are a buyer, never buy anything electrical without testing it first.

**Furniture:** (SR) Extremely Warm

Furniture items are strong sellers at garage sales, provided you can successfully match the right piece with the right person. Furniture-buyers are very choosy. They expect the item to be in perfect condition and yet offered at a very reduced price. The only time customers don't mind having to restore something is when it is an antique or a very unusual piece. A low price is still expected for furniture, however.

**Upholstered furniture** should be clean in order to get a decent price. If the piece does have stains on it, a buyer will not know if they can be successfully removed or not and will usually decide against buying unless they plan to put a slip cover on it anyway. To get the best prices, you should always clean, polish, paint, patch, and repair all furniture items. Or put them out with a "give-away" price on them!

**Children's and baby furniture** is about the only furniture that's a sure seller regardless of condition. If customers know about the crib or playpen you have for sale from your ad, they'll be on your doorstep first thing, the morning of the garage sale. Most people will paint and repair baby furniture to ensure safety of the item and the paint used.

SOMETIMES IT'S BETTER TO DEMONSTRATE
SALE ITEMS YOURSELF.

## Bedding and linens: (SR) lukewarm

Blankets, sheets, pillowcases, towels, and pillows sell reasonable well, if they are clean and in good condition. If you want a decent price for these items, repair any rips or tears. Bedding is a personal item, and buyers are understandably very picky.

If things are faded, that's okay for high-end, quality bedding. But bedding shouldn't be worn thin or stained. Price is very important: $3 to $5 for a blanket or bedspread, depending on size, quality and thickness, $1 to $3 for sheets, depending on size, condition and whether or not they're in sets; $4 for a matched set of twin bed items (two bottoms, two tops, and two pillow cases); $3 to $5 for a matched set of double bed items (one bottom, one top, two pillow cases); $4 to $6 for a similar set for a queen or king-size bed. Bed pillows go for about $1 to $3 each. Down pillows go for $2 to $6. Prices also depend on the quality of the bedding. Is it expensive perma-press percale or just cotton muslin?

Large bath towels still in good condition will sell for about $.50 to $2; regular size towels for about $.25 to $1 depending on condition. Beach towels $.25 to $2.

IT'S NOT MUCH FUN TO BUY OR SELL FROM A DISORGANIZED TABLE.

## Adult clothing

Men's shirts: (SR) Hot!

Formal shirts and men's suits: (SR) Warm

The best sellers in adult clothing are men's casual button-down, polo and tee shirts, long or short sleeve shirts. The standard price is $ .50 to $2 depending on condition. Be sure the shirts are repaired, clean (no stains) and have all their buttons. Also, always indicate their size.

Men's jackets or coats: (SR) Warm (don't even think about getting more than $5 each) Dress, suit and sports jackets ($7 to $10 if their good quality and look near new).

## Large appliances: (SR) Very Warm

These are refrigerators, freezers, stoves, televisions, washers, and dryers. Appliances are solid, but sometimes slow sellers. If you follow the procedure for small appliances: clean them, polish them and make sure that they work. Remember, if an item doesn't work, be honest and tell your buyer it has problems!

## Sports equipment: (SR) Very Warm

These items should be clean, in good condition, and in working order if you want to get back some of the money you invested in them. Fishing gear, camping equipment, bicycles, baseball bats and gloves, footballs, and even small boats and motors are all popular at garage sales. Their popularity does decrease, however, the later into summer you try to sell them. Offer them at a time when people can still envision a little use for their money.

Incidentally, there's no law against selling autos, RV's, trail bikes, ATV's, camping trailers, truck campers, motorcycles, truck shells, boats and things like that at your garage sale. Even your house, if it's for sale that is. Have an OPEN HOUSE the same day you're having your garage sale. Who knows, you just might find a buyer.

## Dishes, glassware, pots and pans: (SR) lukewarm to sizzling

When are dishes and glassware just lukewarm sellers? When they are not in sets. But individual pots and baking dishes, in good condition always sell pretty fast.

When glassware is a real sizzler? When they are in complete sets or single very unique collectable pieces or Depression Glass.

Highly sought-after items include large punch bowls, hand-painted plates, and unique, attractive flower vases. If you are lucky enough to have any Depression-era glass—glass dishes and glassware predating world war II (1941)—you have some very hot collectors' items. Do not sell any old glass until you are certain of its age and value. There are a number of books available that can help you identify and appraise your pieces. Or, for a small fee, most antique dealers will appraise your glassware. And don't forget, if you have any old glassware, mention it in your ad. Collectors will show up in droves!

## Old bottles: (SR): don't bother to sizzling:

Don't bother trying to sell empty bottles unless they are real old. Put them in the city recycle can. And even if they are old, you don't really have a collector's item on your hands unless it's pre-1920 era glass. Prior to the '20s, glass was made using additives, such as lead. These additives, which are no longer contained in glass, food bottles, and medicine bottles, would cause the bottles to turn (change color) when left in bright, direct sunlight. the colors vary and include pale yellow, soft lavender, powder blue, and also deep, passionate purple or solid cobalt blue.

If you think you have a pre-1920 glass bottle, it's very easy to check. You can set it in a safe, secure place outdoors where it can get lots of sunlight. Some people put them on the roof of their houses, but I put my bottles on the ledge of a very high skylight.

Turning takes months to complete so be very, very patient. After about six months, you can check for color, depending on the shade of color you desire. The deeper the color, the better.

Besides the ability to turn, there are other characteristics you can look for that will help determine the age and value of glass bottles: Embossed letters on the side or bottom or embossed numbers on the glass, for example. These make it easier for an expert to identify the bottles. Any bottle in perfect condition (no chips, cracks, or stains) with embossed markings that has turned to a deep, lustrous color is a real collector's item. Even the chipped ones are worth something if they've turned. Tops or stoppers and readable paper labels also add to the value. The last time I checked, old bottles were going for several dollars and could demand much more depending on their age and features.

Author's note: antique and collectibles dealers depend upon the general public to build up their stock. They prowl around garage sales, hoping to pick up valuable items for a song. If you have old collectibles or antiques, learn about them. Don't let someone else make a fortune with your "junk." I almost sold a valuable antique train set for pennies, but luckily a friend advised me to check out its value first. I decided to take his advice. Instead of $20, I sold the set for $175. It pays to be sure.

## Books (SR): warm to Hot:

Hardcover and papers books sell reasonably well, but only if you know how to price them. It doesn't matter what the book cost when it was new, and it doesn't matter that it still looks new. The average hardcover sells for around $1 or $2. Paperbacks go for about 25¢ to 50¢. Educational books (college texts, how-to books, home improvement books, etc.) Will sell well at about half the cover price.

In the case of very old books, check with an antique dealer or bookstore to determine their market value.

Items of adult clothing that move like snails are men's suits and women's formal dresses. No one gives a tinker's darn that you paid more than a $100 for a dress or $200 for a custom tailored man's suit. About the only thing that garage sale customers care about is that all items go for 10 cents on the dollar or less, and that's that! Be sure you really want to sell an expensive, designer dress or man's suit, knowing that the price you might get for it could be very discouraging.

At one of my garage sales, I decided to sell the dress I wore for my daughter's wedding. It had been custom-made and obviously worn only once. I displayed it, along with the matching hat and purse, offering the set at $65 (far less than half the original cost). Well, the offers came rolling in: $15, $20, $25, and finally a whopping $30, if I'd throw in the matching shoes! Being rather new to the game, I didn't realize that the price I was asking was much too high. It was a good deal but not the kind of good deal garage-sale goers expect. I kept the dress. (Later, a good friend talked me out of it for $50 . . . I threw in the matching hat, purse and shoes.

My rule for selling adult clothing is be willing to part with it for peanuts or plan on keeping it.

## Arts and crafts at a Garage Sale? (SR): Cold, warm to Hot:

The term garage sale makes average buyers think of only one thing: BARGAINS. And that's exactly what 99 percent of the folks at your garage sale will be looking for.

If you're into arts and crafts, you'll have a hard time selling them at a garage sale. It has been my experience that you can't get what your beautiful handmade items are worth in such a bargain-price environment. Arts and crafts should always be sold separately, for the fairest prices.

Lovely, handmade items are very popular, though. But if you are going to put all that time and effort into their design, it's only right that you do them justice. Namely, a show of their own. That is the only way to get the prices you want and deserve.

I enjoy oil painting, making crafts out of wood, and creating silk flower arrangements. My crafts sell beautifully at craft and boutique shows, art festivals, in gift shops, and by special order, yet they always seem to be overlooked at garage sales. Remember, the proper type of showplace is the key to selling arts and crafts items. Garage sales are not the best place to show them off, unless you want to sell them for 50% off.

## Home Baked sale items: (SR)Risky

A few words to the wise, stay away from selling any kind of home-cooked food unless you have a license to sell food to the public. Outdoors especially there is just too much risk of food poisoning. The only things in the food category that seem to be a safe bet are canned soda pop, coffee, bakery doughnuts, and packaged popcorn or cookies. for safety and easy clean-up, use only disposable cups, plates, and utensils. Most garage-sale goers are understandable leery of home-baked or canned foods, so save those for the church bazaar or the school fundraiser.

What about those excess store-bought canned goods or packaged foods? Pack them up in boxes and donate them to your church or charity organization. It's better to feel like a million than make a few extra bucks, anyway. And it's tax deductible.

The only sure-fire sellers at a garage sale, food-wise, are extra home-grown fruits and vegetables. But do be sure to check your local zoning and merchant regulations before you open up a full-fledged produce stand.

# More On Products

Before you start tearing hearth and home—and garage—apart looking for all those "priceless" goodies that are just begging to be the stars of your garage sale—and, before you start spending all that green stuff that you're going to make—there are a few extremely important points that you must keep in mind (especially if this is your first venture into garage-selling).

## Point #1

Garage sales, parking lot sales, flea markets, bazaars, yard sales, estate sales and auctions, tag sales, swap meets . . . no matter what you call them, they've been around since the beginning of humanity and will always be here. They are a necessary, useful, practical and enjoyable profession to be a part of, either buying or selling. Everyone loves to buy or sell a bargain. It's the second oldest profession in the world. (hmm . . . sounds like I'm talking about the world's oldest profession, doesn't it?)

## Point #2

A reliable garage-seller is not in the junk business. Our goal is to offer our friends and neighbors useful, reusable, workable items in decent-to-mint condition and at very reasonable and affordable prices.

## Point #3

Don't even consider selling any items that require major repairs by you or the buyer to get them in usable or workable condition. Repairs and/or restoration will probably cost you more than the item is worth.

## Point #4

A little paint here, a little oil on a squeaky hinge there, a scrub brush here, and a little furniture polish there can go a long, long way. Good old elbow grease and spit-polish is the best and cheapest way to go. If it takes any more than that, it's usually precious time and good money down the drain.

## Point #5

As a garage-seller, always remember this very important point: buyers buy first with their eyes and last with their wallets.

## Point #6

Never, ever touch a piece of furniture that may be an antique. Antiques are the only things that sell no matter what they look like, and knowledgeable buyers will want to do the restoration themselves, anyway.

## Point #7 . . . Last but not least.

Garage sales are for making money, right? If items are in need of expensive major repairs, never waste your time trying to sell them. Give them to someone or a charity willing to do the needed repairs or fix it up yourself, then, after an item has paid for its repairs with extended use, you can sell it. If it's beyond repair, break it up and toss the recyclables pieces in your recycle bin. That way, everybody wins.

REMEMBER... MEMORY VALUE ISN'T PART OF THE MARKET VALUE.

IF YOU'RE SHY ABOUT ASKING
NEIGHBORS FOR GARAGE SALE DONATIONS,
THERE ARE OTHER WAYS...

# CHAPTER 12

## Pricing your merchandise

Pricing your goodies is very easy. Just keep in mind that your products should be . . .

1) **Visible:**

Mark the price of every item on a very readable, highly visible label of some kind. A pinned-on piece of paper, a tag with a string or wire to attach it, or an adhesive label all work well. If you prefer you can make a sign that states the price of all the items in a particular box or on a specific table. However, problems can arise at the checkout table. And don't forget all price markings should be large and bold enough to be seen by the near-blind.

2) **Reasonable:**

When you have had something hanging around the ol' homestead for eons, it's very likely that you have become attached to it. When you put it up for sale, remember no one but you gives a hoot about its sentimental value. A ten-dollar item may have a thousand dollars' worth of memories, that's true. But your buyer is buying the item, not your memories.

3) **Flexible:**

Your prices should not be so high that one look turns off a buyer. Think of reasonable, low prices, then add a little room for dickering. This way you'll always be pleased with the price you do get, and the buyer will have had the pleasure of dickering your price down.

4) **Honest:**

Price broken items low and don't try to hide their damage. To the best of your abilities, be sure that damaged items are repairable before you sell them. If a product works and it is electric, have an extension cord handy so that it can be tested. If your prices are good, you will sell lots and lots without resorting to selling faulty items.

The bottom line is that after your first garage sale, you'll want to have another and another and another. you'll need to gain and keep your local buyer's trust.

# CHAPTER 13

## When to Have Your Garage Sale

### The Weather:

Of course it goes without saying (but I'll say it anyway. The weather is the most important factor in deciding when and where you can have your garage sale. It's true that some people will TREK through ten feet of snow to get to a garage sale. Most people won't, however, so try to plan it for a decent weekend. Sometimes the weatherman will give you a bum steer, but do take heart, I have stood in a rainstorm dickering with a buyer as though it was a clear, sunny day, and I had one of my best selling days, ever. You never know.

### The Stars And Moon:

If you're into astrology, then don't forget to check your horoscope prior to your garage sale. The moon is also a consideration. I don't know why, but you get some very strange buyers around dusk on the night of a full moon. Beware.

## The Schedule:

There are other things to consider besides the weather and the stars. For example, it's a good idea to check around to see if there are any important community events scheduled that may steal the crowds from your garage sale. Holiday weekends that take people out of town are also notorious for this.

Also watch out for school or fundraising flea markets. These events, like church bazaars and such, can also reduce your number of eager customers. Check with your neighbors too, because someone else may be planning a garage sale. If so, see if they'll consider sharing the venture and turn it into a block sale. (this allows you to share advertising and set-up costs.

## The Economy:

Garage sales are about as recession-proof as any business could be. In fact, they tend to enjoy more success in tough times.

Time your sales to happen on weekends or just after the first or fifteenth of the month. Pension and Social Security checks come on the first and salaries pay off on the first and the fifteenth. Of course Saturday is good for a few dollars from Friday paychecks.

Now, this all may sound a bit devious, but what good are customers if they 're broke? Conversation? That I can get at the beauty parlor

# CHAPTER 14

## You Don't Have A Garage?!

**Apartment Garage Sales:**

If you live in an apartment, there's really no problem. You simply get together with a few of your apartment neighbors and buddies and have a co-op yard sale. (Don't forget to check with the manager first. Chances are good that he or she will want to throw a few things in to sell too.) If there is a central court in your complex and you can get approval, that's the perfect place. Carports lined up side by side in an accessible location also work great.

Another possibility is to ask a close friend or relative to lend you their garage, yard, or driveway for a day or weekend. Promise them that, for their generosity, you will be happy to sell their excess household item for them and clean up afterward. What an offer! How could they refuse?

If you're feeling real ambitious, you can organize a super-biggie co-op sale at your apartment complex and have everybody bring something to sell (for a small fee). The advertising would read, "Bluebird Apts. Co-op Flea Market, [date & time]" Trust me, having a big, old-fashioned country flea market, get-togethers are a total blast. Oh, and if you don't want to call it a flea market, call it a country bazaar instead. Calling it a bazaar allows you to sell a wider variety of things, including homemade crafts

## The Mobile Home Park Garage Sale:

What about the folks who live in mobile home parks? Yes, you can have a garage sale in your car-port or the park's recreation room. Ask your park manager. Most MHP (mobile home parks) have tight regulations to ensure the privacy, tranquility, and sanity of their inhabitants. Strict regulations, in most cases, are meant to discourage garage sales. The reason behind such regulations is to protect those who would not like their park turned into a 'disorganized' public Flea Market with strangers wandering freely everywhere. There is usually very little extra parking space available, and this could cause a huge hassle and a dangerous problem.

Most MHP are designed like miniature towns or villages with many rows or blocks of homes. There is usually only enough room in your space to park one or two cars, yours. The average MHP have a hundred or more mobile homes in residence at all times. That means an average of one to two hundred or more individual (customers) are right there under your very nose. Most garage-sale customers (90%) come from your immediate neighborhood surrounding a garage sale. There's actually no need to advertise your garage sale outside your own MHP. You already have all the potential customers you will ever need right there at your fingertips. If you keep your sale within the confines of your own MHP, you probably won't break any MHP regulation. Ask your manager. Who knows? He or she might go for it if the public will not need to be involved and no one's privacy will be invaded.

## More: The Mobile Home Park Garage Sale:

In areas that have a hot summer climate, garage sales are held mostly in the lush coolness of the evening. Air conditioning or not, everyone heads outdoors the instant the sun disappears behind the hills. In a friendly mobile home village in these areas, the evening atmosphere is aglow with the warmth of an old family get-together when someone decides to have a community garage sale. Maybe only a small group of neighbors, out for their nightly walk in the cool evening air, will stroll by to see all the goodies and try some of your delicious homemade cookies and lemonade. What a nice way to spend a summer evening, and what a pleasant place and time to have a garage sale.

# CHAPTER 15

## Setting up your garage sale, Or Open Air Yard Sales

If you are lucky enough to have a big, uncluttered, two or three car garage in which to have your garage sale, that's amazing, 'cause very few do these days. So, if you do, the opening-day problems of setup, pricing, arranging tables attractively, and the final all-around assessment can be done leisurely the night before, behind closed garage doors. Then, when the big day arrives, all you need do is put up your signs, open the garage door, spread out into the driveway and rake in the dollars!

Merchandise display tables are one of the most important parts of setting up. Many garage sales look more like trash heaps or a junk yard. Items are dumped onto the driveway, strewn around the garage floor or tossed on the lawn. This is not good for business. People get dirty. They can't get a good look at your products, and they can get a backache from all that bending over.

You must have tables or some types of platform to keep things up off the floor or ground where they do not normally belong. A four-by-eight sheet of plywood on two sawhorses covered with a sheet makes a great display table. Beg, borrow, or steal anything that you can make into tables. Always cover your tables with old, clean tablecloths, curtains, sheets, or blankets. Put cardboard boxes under the table covers to raise merchandise up for a better viewing.

The placement of your tables is very important too. Always place them so you can have full view of each table during the action. Also, make sure you leave enough space to allow free movement between and around tables. Shoplifters love easy pickings at a crowded, unorganized, messy garage sales.

If your garage sale cannot be held in your garage, just call it a yard sale. if the weather is nice, a yard sale can be even better. The word yard instead of garage usually makes buyers feel that you have more or bigger items to sell. It will also suggest that there will be lots and lots of goodies available, like there would be at a flea market.

Personally I prefer the open-air yard sales. Buyers do too. Strangers prefer to walk into open yards rather than into someone's private garage. But, if you are planning to have a sale inside your garage, be sure to extend it outside onto your open driveway and yard, being sure to keep everything in your sight at all times. Also make sure that you are in plain sight of the buyers. Be **identifiable and always available. Circulate; Do not hide.**

MUSIC PUTS PEOPLE IN A BUYING MOOD.

## Music makes for a happy garage sale:

High-class establishments offer background music, so why should we garage-sale managers do any differently?

Music soothes the tired mind and body. It lifts the spirit and puts people in a relaxed, buying mood.

My husband hooked up a speaker in our garage so that I could have mood music at all my garage sales. It's a little extra hassle, though worth it sales-wise. If you have a portable radio or stereo, put it out there and turn it on. Be careful where you place it, though. At one of my garage sales, I sold our portable radio by mistake. It was the one I was using for our garage sale music. That's why I now have piped-in music. It would be pretty hard to sell that.

## Decorations at your garage sale:

When you come right down to it, a garage sale is nothing more than a big ol' party. So why not make it look like a party.

Colorful streamers or balloons draped from trees, bright paper party table coverings, and even a little tinsel on hedges and shrubs can really add to the festive mood of your garage sale. Of course you'll spend a little more in terms of cost and clean-up, but could you resist stopping at a brightly decorated garage sale? I save leftover party decorations and I ask friends to do the same. That way I can save a bundle of money on decorations.

A pretty environment makes people feel happier and more relaxed. That means they will be more receptive to the idea of spending money. Also there is a lot of competition in the garage-sale network nowadays. A single block can sometimes have two, three, even four garage sales going on at one time. If one of those sales looks more colorful, the decision of which one to try first is made very easily. Let it be your sale. Decorate!

With so many garage sales...

...you need *special* advertising.
Like...

# CHAPTER 16

## The Principles Of Advertising

Advertising, whether it's for a national product or a local product (like your garage sale), always follows a few basic principles. As you make up you posters, flyers, classified ads, etc., keep these six concepts in mind:

1) **Be unique:** Try to do or say things a little differently.

2) **Be creative:** Try to do something, advertising or sales-wise, that's never been done.

3) **Be assertive:** Be proud of what you're offering and let your ads show it.

   Don't be afraid to approach people to get help with your advertising (store managers, or news editors).

4) **Be specific:** Don't be wishy-washy about what you have to sell. List important items (if you have room).

5) **Be bold:** Of course an ad must get noticed in order to get read. In flyers and posters, use bold colors and lettering.

6) **Be organized:** Do not do your advertising too soon or at the last minute. Find out how local retailers time their sale advertising and follow their example for best results in your area.

## How To Get Free Advertising

It sounds too good to be true, but there really are ways to get free advertising for your garage sale. And you don't have to know the local newspaper editor.

If you live in a small town where not a whole lot happens, then of course a garage sale will be big news. But even if you live in a medium-to-large city, you can still get newspaper—even radio and television—coverage for free.

Every newspaper, large or small, has a daily or weekly local events page. On it you'll find leads about visiting theatre troupes, film festivals, wine-tasting parties, and so on. Your garage sale can be on that list, maybe even rate a little write-up. Here's all you do:

1) Plan your event to be the most fun and exciting sale you can create. Get together with friends and neighbors and have a carnival or other theme party. You can even give away prizes for winning country-fair-type games.

2) Put on a special items sale, a sale that focuses on antiques and collectibles, furniture, fine women's clothing, children's toys

and clothing, home repair materials and equipment, or some other specific area of items.

3) Host a garage sale that's at least in part, a fundraiser or charity drive. You can pick a specific group, a local school sports program, girl's club, whatever, or charity, and aim to raise a certain amount or donate so many cents on the dollar.

## Advertising Your Garage Sale

I like to run my ads during the week prior to my garage sale, **not** on the day of the sale, as some folks do. Within the week before my garage sale I put an ad in my weekly Penny Saver, on Craig's List, in our hometown and neighborhood newspaper and circulate flyers among my friends, my neighborhood and post them in the ladies room where I work. My way gives buyers plenty of time to make their shopping plans for the coming weekend.

Your ad should be short and sweet, bold, informative, warm, friendly, and witty. And remember, your ad must appeal to the readers or they will pass up your sale.

The first step, of course, is to get your ad noticed. My rule is simply, **don't be dull**. Avoid using a lot of words. (That can get costly.) Just use the right ones. Don't be afraid to be humorous, entertaining, provocative, or anything else that will get your ad noticed and remembered.

I have made some examples and I invite you to use them. (note: The words Garage Sale need not appear in your ad if the classified section is entitled Garage Sales.)

## MORE ON NEWSPAPER ADVERTISING:

Need some ideas for your successful newspaper or shopping guide ad campaign? Well, get ready 'cause here they come! (all you add is the address, date, and time.)

DIVORCE SALE! HIS LOSS, YOUR GAIN

BEST LITTLE GARAGE SALE IN TOWN . . . WE'VE GOT IT ALL!

ESTATE SALE! ANTIQUES? COULD BE, COME SEE!

3 BLOCK SALE 12 FAMILIES, HUGE VARIETY

CLEANING OUT HOUSE GOT A LOT OF EVERYTHING!

MOVING!!! NEED CASH! MY LOSS YOUR GAIN!

SPRING CLEANING . . . FIVE SPRINGS BEHIND! GREAT BARGAINS!

FOUR SPORTS WIDOWS' SELLING ASSORTED MACHO-TOYS, VIDEO GAMES & [UNUSED] EXCERSIZE EQUIPMENT.

HUBBIE GROWS UP! SELLING HIS OLD TOYS!

DISTRESS SALE TOO MUCH STUFF, TOO LITTLE ROOM!

DIVORCE SALE: NEVER USED DIY TOOLS! CHEAP!

## TIP:

Once you've decided on the type of sale you're going to host, the next step is to inform the media. Who you should contact varies, but at a newspaper, the city (local news) editor or entertainment editor is usually your best bet. At a radio or TV station, you can send a press release to the station manager, public affairs (public relations) manager, or directly to your favorite newsperson or disc jockey. All, I might add, will respond much more favorably to a charity garage sale.

TO CRAFT A PRESS RELEASE, In addition to a brief, cordial, to-the-point letter, you should include the following information on a separate sheet:

1) date and time.

2) location.

3) type of sale (antique, carnival, charity, etc.).

4) type of items at the sale, type of games and activities, type/ name of charity to be benefited.

5) lots of adjectives describing the sales items or theme, or the accomplishments of the charity.

6) a repeat of date and location.

Note: If your release is to be read on the air, type it in all CAPS, DOUBLE-SPACED.

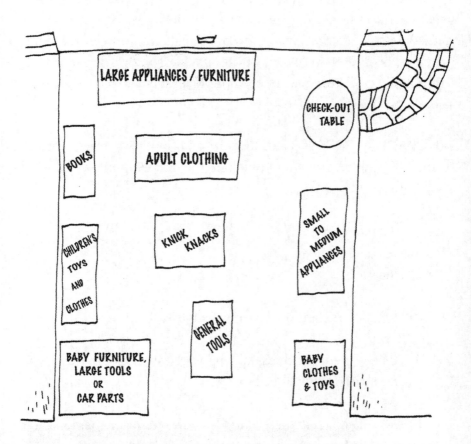

THE DRIVEWAY SALE: HOT ITEMS UP FRONT!

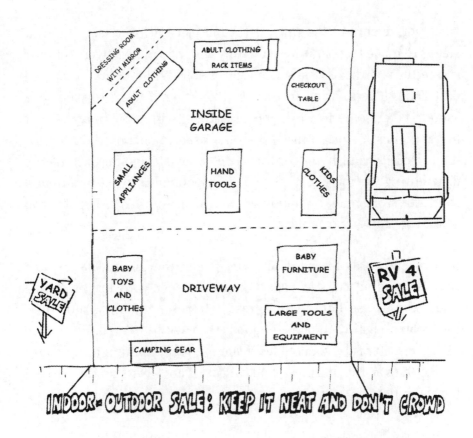

DRESSING ROOM WITH MIRROR

ADULT CLOTHING

ADULT CLOTHING RACK ITEMS

CHECKOUT TABLE

INSIDE GARAGE

SMALL APPLIANCES

HAND TOOLS

KIDS CLOTHES

BABY TOYS AND CLOTHES

DRIVEWAY

BABY FURNITURE

LARGE TOOLS AND EQUIPMENT

CAMPING GEAR

YARD SALE

RV 4 SALE

INDOOR - OUTDOOR SALE: KEEP IT NEAT AND DON'T CROWD

## Flyers:

The classifieds section is great for getting to those people already looking for garage sales. But how do you reach those hundreds of potential shoppers who don't regularly check the paper? With flyers . . . duh!

Once you're sure of the time, date, and place of your sale, the next step is to make lots of funny, cute, silly and informative flyers on your computer and make lots of copies. The job should be fun, easy and cost little. Flyers, bring in the neighbors. Send them to your kids school, takes some to work and send them with your hubby. Don't forget to post or pass out your flyers, head to shopping centers or malls close to your home (or the site of your sale, if different). Before distributing your flyers, it is of course a good idea to get permission from the store manager or other individual in charge. Usually you won't run into any trouble.

Now a few words to the wise about flyers: they should be printed on eye-catching colored paper, or white paper with bright colors. They should use bold, easy-to-read lettering, and they should be informative, listing the type of goods that will be offered. Be sure to list special items or collectibles if you are lucky enough to have any. Collectibles are big business, and collectors are always on the lookout for bargains.

It makes a lot of sense to include a map on your flyers and phone number (optional) if you think that further instructions or information might be needed. Your flyers must be clean (no ink smudges) and organized too, because this is a reflection of the kind of garage sale you'll be hosting. Do not, however, make your flyers look like you had Michelangelo make them. People will get the idea that you'll be charging high prices.

# 4-FAMILY YARD SALE

**SAT. (only) SEPT. 25TH 9AM-7PM**

## Featuring:

- ☆ TOOLS!
- ☆ FURNITURE!
- ☆ APPLIANCES!
- ☆ KID'S TOYS!

- ☆ SPORTS EQUIP.
- ☆ ELECTRONICS
- ☆ CAMPING GEAR
- ☆ KID'S CLOTHES!

123-456-789

1421 OAK LOOP
SAN JOSE (JUST
NORTH OF DOWNTOWN)

## BE THERE!

## THE PERFECT POSTER
FLIER OR SIGN

## Posters:

Posters are a very important part of your advertising plan. For best results make them big and bold, and place them at nearby busiest intersections.

You can make posters from poster board, a heavy paper product that's available in any school, office, or art supply store. You can also construct posters out of large pieces of flat cardboard covered with white shelf paper. Poster paints, large, dark-color felt pens or wide markers work great. Or, at a home store you can buy large, pre-printed, waterproof Garage Sale signs that you can reuse for sale after sale.

I learned the hard way that the most important thing on a poster is an arrow, especially if you live in a neighborhood where garage sales are plentiful. And, provide more arrows along the way so you can lead people right to your garage sale. Of course directly beneath these arrows should be the words garage sale and your address (on the more distant signs).

Using heavy tape, attach your signs securely to street sign poles, telephone poles, etc., so that they won't flap in the breeze, blow away, or just drop off. These perils are why I prefer to use heavy cardboard covered with white shelf paper for my posters. They're sturdy and inexpensive, and if secured right, they don't flap or fall off.

Do go check your signs periodically during the day. One afternoon, all of a sudden people stopped coming to my garage sale. I went to check on the signs and, sure enough, they had ripped off the poles and were face down in the street. The next time I avoided this by using heavy duct tape that had to be cut off after the sale was over.

Always remember to take down your posters and signs immediately after your garage sale closes. If you don't, people will keep bothering you, thinking that now you'll be desperate enough to make killer deals on items that you didn't sell.

But mainly, there is nothing tackier than seeing old, tattered, ragged garage-sale signs dangling from telephone poles. It gives all garage sellers a bad name, and in some cities it's illegal and the owner can be fined for littering. So if you have your address on the signs, or even if you don't, heed this warning and always take down all your advertising after your sale is over.

Billy
the thinker

Lukie
the lover

Ricky
the joker

Suzy
lil' mama hen

MY SCAVENGER SQUAD
(BLESS THEIR LITTLE HEARTS!)

# CHAPTER 17

## Getting The Kids Into The Act

When my three oldest boys were eight, ten, and twelve, and my daughter Sue was four, they all decided they wanted to have a flea market in our front yard. At first I was a little leery of the idea, but when the kids pleaded their case, I became convinced that this adventure would indeed make money, not to mention and a precious memory. I agreed to the scheme, since my kitchen window overlooked the front yard, I would have a clear view of their entire operation.

As soon as they got the okay for their flea market, away they went. First they attacked their bedrooms: drawers, closets, and toy boxes were shown no mercy. They filled bags and boxes as fast as they could find them. My head was in a constant spin just trying to keep an eye on what was going outside the front door.

Then the kids made crude but effective signs, put up a big table, made of wooden and cardboard boxes, planks and proceeded to display their merchandise. The word went out like lightning. In no time at all, my poor front yard looked like freebie day at Disneyland. It was amazing! I didn't know there were that many children in our entire neighborhood! My kids even got me into the act by getting me to make lemonade for them—which they then sold to thirsty and desperate junior patrons for a nickel a paper cup. It was really quite a profitable afternoon.

Around dinnertime I asked the kids to start cleaning up, though I really hated to foreclose on their thriving business.

"How'd it go? Make a lot of sales?" I asked my little merchants.

"We sold everything," Bill, my oldest answered, "except for the real junk. We'll just throw that away."

Behind Billy, I could see Lukie, my middle son, tallying up his last big sale.

Later after the clean-up, I noticed someone rushing past the kitchen door.

"Where are you going with that box full of stuff?" I yelled from the kitchen as Ricky, my youngest, struggled across the family room headed for his bedroom. "I thought you guys said you sold all the good stuff. That sure looks like good stuff to me."

"We did sell everything." He grunted under the weight of the heavy box he was carrying. "This stuff's . . . on layaway."

"Oh, well, excuse me, mr. Big business." I laughed. "I hope you got deposits on all that good stuff."

"Oh, mom," Ricky sighed, shifting his heavy load.

"We got deposits," said Lukie, who was following close behind.

"See, here's our list," Billy, my oldest said, handed me a smudged and wrinkled piece of paper. "we wrote down everything."

I stared in total amazement at that scrap of paper. It was a masterpiece! It listed every item, who brought it, how much each person put down on it, and the balance they owed. For example, "bobby: baseball bat, 25¢—paid 13¢, still owes 12¢," and so on, and on.

Footnote:

During the next few weeks, each time the list was hauled out, the items were either marked 'PAID' and handed over to its new owner, or a few more hard-earned pennies were deducted from the outstanding balance. This went on until every single item was paid for and picked up. I wonder if grown-up merchants can boost the same success rate. What a great memory! Eat your heart out, Donald Trump!

## Getting The Kids Into The Act
## Part Two

Their appetites whet with a delicious taste of high finance, my fearless foursome decided that they were ready for the big time: Our local Flea Market. Which was the largest in the SF Bay Area. I gave my okay, once again, so never let it be said that I'd ever stand in the way of progress. (actually, I was hoping that they'd just forget all about it.)

The split second after those words of permission slipped through my lips, my "scavenger squad" set about scavenging items for their big sale. Anything inside or outside the house that wasn't nailed down was subject to sudden disappearance. My darling four-year-old daughter Sue-Sue's vocabulary, which was quite extensive up until then, was suddenly reduced to five pitiful words: "Mommy, can I sell this?"

As the big day drew closer, I began to realize that this was going to result in either the fondest of memories or the worst headache of all time. The goings-on were taking on a kind of comical tone as the scavenger squad found itself subjected to frequent line-ups and body searches. Paper bags, sacks, and boxes—all filled until their seams threatened to give—began to crowd the rooms and hallways of our house. I couldn't imagine where all the stuff was coming from and fully expected to discover a 'charity donation center' sign posted in the front yard.

At last the big day arrived and we were all up at dawn packed and ready to head for the open air flea market, not yet knowing that the kids had picked the hottest day ever recorded for the month of July in our area. By the end of the day I was convinced that we would all look like barbecued chicken.

We were assigned a spot and the kids set their tables up individually because they wanted to sell their own stuff at their own prices. It's funny, but a lot of the stuff they were selling sure looked like things I used to own.

During the day the sun kept getting hotter and the crowd kept getting bigger—and the "squad" kept getting richer. If anyone came within six feet of our spot, they were lured in like a fish on a line. They were doomed. No one got away.

The wheeling and dealing was a huge kick to watch. Little Sue got into the act right along with her big brothers. Her table was of course the lowest and smallest with the least amount of goodies to sell, but she was not to be outdone. In no time at all, her pennies, nickels, and dines began to stack up. After about two hours, she asked me to count her "monies" for her and we tallied up a whopping $1.10, which was plenty for a four-year old's shopping spree.

She had already spotted a tricycle across the isle at another sale that she loved with all her heart. She took her small fortune and after much dickering with an old man who owned it, she proudly bought the rolling disaster for seventy-five cents. It was a squeaking, screeching, rusted wreck, but she was very proud of her purchase and I was proud of my blossoming little businesswoman.

The boys were having as much fun as Sue, and I couldn't believe how fast they were selling things. Their prices were fair, so fair in fact that I was in a state of swooning at some of the deals they were making. The rascals were even buying things from each other, then, when the other wasn't looking, they'd resell the items for more than they'd paid their own brother! I tried to intervene once in a while, but the answer was always the same: "hey, business is business, mom!"

By the end of the day, it was obvious that the big flea market adventure had been a huge success to say the least. There would of course be many more sales, as the scavenger squad grew up, to add to the family's list of memories and stories.

(The saga of Sue-Sue's famous squeaky tricycle remained a favorite, even after the trike developed quite a nasty habit of trying to escape on the back of the weekly garbage truck. [when it was left outside on the sidewalk overnight] Even after frequent rescues from the truck by her brothers, one day it succeeded and we never saw it again.)

So, from my own book of priceless memories I can highly recommend that you let the kids get into the garage sale act. Trust me, you will create many priceless memories, too.

# CHAPTER 18

## Multi-Family And Group Garage Sales

### Profit and Labor-Sharing:

The only drawback to a large family or group garage sale is that the workload sometimes gets unevenly distributed, or unevenly performed.

The best way to make sure everyone does their share—and consequently earns their share of the profits—is to assign tasks or responsibilities. For example, one couple could be in charge of decorations: bring the streamers and tinsel and put it all up. One couple could paint a few posters, and then another couple could go out and post them. One couple could set up the tables, another could take them down, and another could sweep the driveway afterward. Oh, and the kids could go to the local supermarket and pass out flyers or help with some other simple task.

With the preceding plan, when somebody sells an item, everyone else will have played an equal, supportive, neighborly role in helping them sell it.

## Creating a Workable Sales System:

When more than one family of fun-loving people get together to put on a really big show, that's when the fun really begins. This type of garage sale is my favorite. But, in all the excitement, with merchandise from several families, how can you keep things straight?

The idea came to me one day while I was at work. I have worked in the electronics industry for twenty years, and in that business your life revolves around the color-code system. That's how everything is controlled and categorized. I knew that color-coding would be the perfect way to keep us sellers from wondering what belongs to whom when a customer takes a product off the table and heads for the checkout counter.

The first thing to do is assign each family a color. I give them each matching stickers, labels, and paper. I'm always yellow, the color of GOLD! If colored stickers, labels, and paper are not available, white pieces of paper and a box of crayons or felt pens will do the job, very inexpensively too.

When one family needs to leave the sale for any reason, there is never a real problem, because all their items are color-coded. When any of their items are sold, the money goes into their envelope (also color-coded). Believe me, this method can really simplify life at the big group garage sale.

## The Successful, Super-Fun Garage Sale: A Case Study

"We, the garage sellers of America, salute you!"

I have been looking for the perfect garage sale for a long, long time. Some have come pretty darn close, let me tell you. But others, I am sorry to say, were so tacky that I was ashamed that they were even called garage sales! "Useless Junk Sale" would have been more appropriate. That is one of the main reasons I decided to write a book. I love to hold and go to garage sales, and everyone I know feels the same way, so I felt that the proud ol' tradition of garage-selling deserved a few simple guidelines.

My biggest pet peeve is, as I mentioned, is a useless junk sale masquerading as an honorable garage sale, and there is nothing I am more delighted by than a well-organized, neat, clean, fun, garage sale that offers repaired, clean, reusable items.

Some dear friends of ours are garage-sale nuts. They have always had one big garage sale a year rather than several small ones. As the years went by, their once-a-year sale began to grow. First one house, then a few more in their court, then houses from the next block, and so on began to join in with garage sales of their own, until someone wisely suggested that one great big community garage sale extravaganza would be the way to go.

Flyers were sent out to all the neighbors, asking if they would be interested in this co-op venture. Everyone loved the idea. In no time at all, forty families were signed up and ready to go. An ad was put into the newspaper so the whole south bay area knew about it. Each participating family donated $5 for the newspaper ad, the flyers, maps and for colored balloons, [a different color each year] to mark the participating homes.

I arrived on the morning of the first extravaganza sale and was amazed to say the least. I could feel the excitement building around me as I entered the neighborhood. There were balloons and big garage sale signs everywhere you looked. People were hustling and bustling, chirping and chattering all over the place. It felt like big family carnival.

In no time at all, the streets were filled with friendly strangers with trucks, carts and wagons in tow, or big tote bag just begging to be filled.

Right off, it was apparent to yours truly the 'expert,' that here at last, was a group that had done everything right garage-sale-wise.

#1  They chose to have a co-op rather than compete with each other.

#2  They shared the expenses of advertising.

#3  They shared the work of organizing and advertising.

#4  Signs were posted in the most effective places.

#5  On the morning of the sale, additional maps and flyers were distributed at the entrances to the neighborhood.

#6  All homes offered high-quality, clean, working merchandise.

#7  They offered refreshments to the hot, tired, and thirsty.

#8  All signs, flyers, and ads were informative, attractive, and instructive.

#9 They chose a perfect time, mid September, to have their once-a-year garage sale. The weather was comfortable and yet still predictable.

If you host a garage sale like this one, then I might soon be saluting you.

# CHAPTER 19

## The Legal Side
### [the dull boring stuff]

## Legal Aspects Of Neighborhood Merchandising

Just so that this guide would be complete, I had my attorney, Charles T. Kilian, write a few words on the legal aspects of neighborhood merchandising.

Anyways people, here it is . . .

## Liability

I am assuming that neighborhood merchandising is occurring in and around someone's residence. Normally that person would have comprehensive homeowner's insurance. I think it is important that this form of insurance not be solely relied on to provide coverage in case of liability to a third party. If someone comes on the premises for the purpose of shopping at a garage sale and incurs some sort of injury as a result thereof, the owner probably would be covered under the owner's homeowner's policy. Normally, with respect to liability, the homeowner's policy covers any and all claims made against the property owner, with certain specified exclusions. It is important to check the homeowner's policy to make certain that a garage sale is not excluded from coverage. In addition, if neighborhood merchandising is occurring on a regular basis, the insurance company may take the position on a regular basis, the insurance company may take the position that this is an actual business rather than an occasional attempt by a homeowner to sell surplus goods. If a person intents to have neighborhood merchandising on a regular basis at the same location, it is my feeling that he or she should investigate obtaining a separate business policy for that purpose, even though the homeowner's policy may cover in individual cases.

## Taxes

Obviously any neighborhood merchandising is a business and any income derived there from must be reported to the internal revenue service and state franchise tax board by the person earning the income. The real question is whether a person who works at such a garage sale is subject to the withholding of their wages. For years employers have utilized individuals as independent contractors without being required to withhold. The internal revenue service and the state labor commission have both cracked down on what they consider abuse of this process. According to IRS and labor commission guidelines, if an employer has "control" over an employee, then that person is an employee for purposes of withholding. Hence, if an individual is seeking to accomplish neighborhood merchandising on a regular basis, he or she should be prepared to withhold for employees.

## Zoning and permits

With respect to zoning and permits, the state of California has not preempted the field of regulation of neighborhood merchandising. Hence, local jurisdictions (cities and countries) have the right, and in many cases have exercised that right, to regulate garage sales. Therefore, anyone contemplating neighborhood merchandising should inquire into the local jurisdiction's rule and regulations, if any, regarding neighborhood merchandising. Even if there is no specific ordinance regulating garage sales, many local agencies may take the position that neighborhood merchandising, especially accomplished on a large, ongoing scale, constitutes a business that is in violation of the city's residential zoning ordinance. I do not believe that this is a problem for one-time or occasional garage sales, absent a local regulation specifically regulating them; however, an ongoing sale may result in violation of the city's residential zoning ordinance. Many cities have adopted home occupation ordinances that allow certain types of businesses or occupations to be commenced or to be continued in the home. In my research i have not found any cities that have specifically allowed garage sales or neighborhood merchandising as a home occupation. One who wishes to operate in a city or country on a regular basis should also apply to that local agency for a business license, since any type of business, even if a home occupation, are usually subject to the business license provisions of local ordinances.

In summary, any person wishing to consider operating a continuing or large-scale neighborhood merchandising business out of a home should:

1. Check the relevant homeowner's insurance policy to see that there are no exclusions;

2. In any event, obtain a separate business liability insurance policy;

3. Consider withholding from employee's wages federal and state income tax and other taxes required to be withheld;

4. Check with their local jurisdiction to see what regulations, if any, would prohibit the operation of an ongoing business out of the home.

# CONCLUSION

As the sun sets peacefully in garage-sale land

I truly hope that, in my own small way, I have made an impression on your life, in the form of enlightenment or simple enjoyment.

The methods outlined in this book are drawn from my own profitable experiences, and they really work. You can put them to money making use as soon as the weather and your workers are willing.

If you live with a pack rat and you want to have a garage sale, remember to approach the subject very carefully. Open up the discussion gently and quietly, with a few, carefully chosen words, like:

"Hey, listen you! I'm tired of this mess! It looks like a city dump around here and I'm gonna do something about it once and for all . . . I'm gonna have the biggest garage sale since God made dirt and get rid of all this 'stuff.' I'm gonna sell it all . . . just watch me!!" Oops, sorry, I got a little carried away there.

Back to what I was saying.

The important thing to do is to get your pack rat and other reluctant members of your clan to realize that you all truly need the money and the sanity of a less cluttered, clean house (and lay that old guilt trip on real thick).

Throughout this book I've heaped a lot of blame on the poor hoarders and pack rats of the world. But I honestly don't know what we garage-sale moguls would do without them. We wouldn't have a single thing to sell, that's for certain. And even though they can turn your living room, bedroom, patio, garage, back porch, and so on, into what resembles the 7th redneck infantry's obstacle course, we must still find room in our hearts (the little devils even burrow their way in there.) to love 'em. I still love mine and always will—so, what else could I do? Murder is still considered a capital offence in this state.